lonely planet

# Lao

## Phrasebook & Dictionary

## Acknowledgments

**Product Editor** Andrea Dobbin
**Book Designer** Mazzy Prinsep
**Language Writer** Joe Cummings
**Cover Image Researcher** Naomi Parker

## Thanks

Bruce Evans, James Hardy, Liz Heynes, Andi Jones, Wayne Murphy, Catherine Naghten, Anthony Phelan, John Taufa, Angela Tinson, Branislava Vladisavljevic, Juan Winata

**Published by Lonely Planet Global Limited**
CRN 554153
6th Edition – Sep 2025
ISBN 9781 8386 9148 6

**Cover Image** Laos, Bolaven Plateau. A monk at Tad Yeung waterfall, Katie Garrod/AWL Images
Printed in Malaysia 10 9 8 7 6 5 4 3 2 1

**Contact** lonelyplanet.com/contact

## about the author

After investing most of his youth strangling Stratocasters in dark bars, Joe Cummings ran away from home with the Peace Corps and discovered South-East Asia. Returning to his native USA, he earned meagre but steady cash as a professional student for several years, gaining two master's degrees, one in South-East Asian Studies/Thai Language and another in Applied Linguistics. He has also worked as a translator/interpreter of Thai, a Lao bilingual consultant in the USA and as a tour guide in Laos. Along the way, Joe hit the road for LP, writing the first editions of LP's *Thailand* and *Laos* guides, which he continues to update regularly. He has also authored LP's *Thai phrasebook, World Food: Thailand* and *Buddhist Stupas of Asia: The Shape of Perfection*. Joe visits Laos frequently from his home base in Thailand.

## from the author

I'm indebted to a Lao friend who helped with the Lao script for this book, but who wished not to be mentioned by name. Thanks also to Steven Schipani, who facilitated many exchanges. For logistical support, I thank Oliver Bandmann of Baan Khily Gallery.

## from the publisher

Special thanks to Manivone Watson for the creation of the Sustainable Travel section.

## make the most of this phrasebook ...

Anyone can speak another language! It's all about confidence. Don't worry if you can't remember your school language lessons or if you've never learnt a language before. Even if you learn the very basics (on the inside covers of this book), your travel experience will be the better for it. You have nothing to lose and everything to gain when the locals hear you making an effort.

## being understood

Throughout this book you'll see coloured phrases on each page. They're phonetic guides to help you pronounce the language. Start with them to get a feel for how the language sounds. The Pronunciation section will explain more, but you can be confident that if you read the coloured phrase, you'll be understood.

## communication tips

Body language, ways of doing things, sense of humour – all have a role to play in every culture. The aside boxes included throughout this phrasebook give you useful cultural and linguistic information that will help you communicate with the locals and enrich your travel experience.

## Lao

For more details, see the **introduction**.

ABOUT LAO

The official language of the Lao People's Democratic Republic (LPDR) is Lao as spoken and written in Vientiane. As an official language, it has successfully become the lingua franca between all Lao and non-Lao ethnic groups in Laos. Of course, native Lao is spoken with differing tonal accents and with slightly differing vocabularies as you move from one part of the country to the next, especially in a north to south direction. But it is the Vientiane dialect that is most widely understood.

Modern Lao linguists recognise four basic dialects within the country: Vientiane Lao; Northern Lao (spoken in Sainyabuli, Bokeo, Udomxai, Phongsali, Luang Nam Tha and Luang Prabang); North-Eastern Lao (Xieng Khuang, Hua Phan), Central Lao (Khammuan, Bolikhamsai); and Southern Lao (Champasak, Salavan, Savannakhet, Attapeu, Sekong). Each of these can be further divided into subdialects; a distinction between the Lao spoken in the neighbouring provinces of Xieng Khuang and Hua Phan, for example, is readily apparent to those who know Lao well.

All dialects of Lao are members of the Thai half of the Thai-Kadai family of languages and are closely related to languages spoken in Thailand, northern Myanmar and pockets of China's Yunnan Province. Standard Lao is indeed close enough to Standard Thai (as spoken in central Thailand) that, for native speakers, the two are mutually intelligible. In fact, virtually all speakers of Lao living in the Mekong River Valley can easily understand spoken Thai, since the bulk of the television and radio they listen to is broadcast from Thailand. Among educated Lao, written Thai is also easily understood, in spite of the fact that the two scripts differ (to about the same degree that the Greek and Roman scripts differ). This is because many of the textbooks used at the college and university level in Laos are actually Thai texts.

Even closer to Standard Lao are Thailand's Northern and North-Eastern Thai dialects. North-Eastern Thai (also called Isan) is virtually 100% Lao in vocabulary and intonation; in fact there are more Lao speakers living in Thailand than in Laos. Hence if you're travelling to Laos after a spell in Thailand (especially the north-east), you should be able to put whatever you learned in Thailand to good use in Laos. It doesn't work as well in the opposite direction; native Thais can't always understand Lao since they've had less exposure.

## abbreviations used in this book

| | | | |
|---|---|---|---|
| **adj** | adjective | **pl** | plural |
| **adv** | adverb | **prep** | preposition |
| **conj** | conjunction | **sg** | singular |
| **lit** | literal translation | **v** | verb |
| **n** | noun | | |

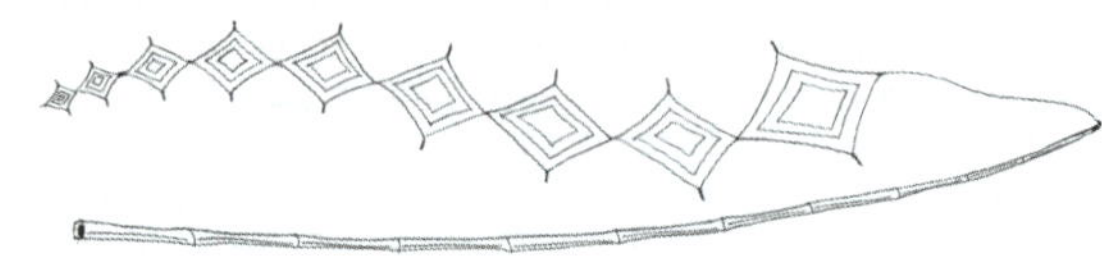

The rendering of Lao words into Roman script is a major problem, as many Lao sounds, especially certain vowels, do not occur in English. The problem is compounded by the fact that, because of Laos' colonial history, transcribed words most commonly seen in Laos are based on the colonial French system of transliteration, which bears little relation to the way an English speaker would usually choose to write a Lao word.

Take, for example, the capital of Laos, Vientiane. The Lao pronunciation, following a fairly logical English transliteration, would be Wieng Chan (some might hear it more as Wieng Jan). The French don't have a written consonant that corresponds to 'w', so they chose to use a 'v' to represent all 'w' sounds, even though the 'v' sound in Lao is closer to an English 'w'. The same goes for 'ch' (or 'j'), which for the French was best rendered 'ti-'; hence Wieng Chan comes out 'Vientiane' in the French transliteration. The 'e' is added so that the final 'n' sound isn't partially lost, as it is in French words ending with 'n'. This latter phenomenon also happens with words like lâan (ລ້ານ, million) as in Lan Xang, which most French speakers would write as 'Lane', a spelling that leads most English speakers to pronounce this word like the 'lane' in 'Penny Lane' (which is way off base).

As there is no official method of transliterating Lao (the Lao government is incredibly inconsistent in this respect, though they tend to follow the old French methods), we have created a transcription system similar to that used in Lonely Planet's Thai phrasebook, since the languages have a virtually identical sound system. The public and private sectors in Laos are gradually moving towards a more internationally recognisable system along the lines of the Royal Thai General Transcription (which is fairly readable across a large number of language types). This can also be problematic, however, as when an 'r' is used where an 'h' or 'l' is the actual sound, simply because the Lao symbols for these sounds look so much like the Thai 'r' (spoken Lao has no 'r' sound). Don't worry though, with our system, you'll be fine.

# vowels

The x in the Lao script indicates the position that a consonant must fill to produce a written syllable.

| vowels | | |
|---|---|---|
| xິ | i | as the 'i' in 'it' |
| xີ | ii | as the 'ee' in 'feet' or 'tea' |
| xະ, xັx | a | as the 'u' in 'fun' |
| xາ | aa | as the 'a' in 'father' |
| ແx | ae | as the 'a' in 'bat' |
| ເxະ, ເxັx | e | as the 'e' in 'hen' |
| ເx | eh | as the 'a' in 'hate' |
| xຸ | u | as the 'u' in 'flute' |
| xູ | uu | as the 'oo' in 'food' |
| xໍ, ອ | aw | as the 'aw' in 'jaw' |
| xຳ | am | ats the 'um' in 'rum' |
| ເxິ, ເxີ | oe | as the 'uh' in 'huh' |
| xຶ, xື | eu | similar to the 'i' in 'sir' or the 'eux' in the French 'deux' |
| **diphthongs** | | |
| ໄx, ໃx | ai | as the 'i' in 'pipe' |
| ເxົາ, xາວ | ao | as the 'ow' in 'now' |
| ໂxະ, xົ | o | as the 'o' in 'phone' |
| ໂx | oh | as the 'o' in 'toe' |
| ເxືອ | eua | combine eu and a |
| ເxັຍ, ເxຍ, xຽx | ia | combine i and a, or the 'ie' in the French 'rien' |
| xົວ | ua | as the 'our' in 'tour' |
| xວຍ | uay | as the 'ewey' in 'Dewey' |
| xິວ | iu | as the 'ew' in 'yew' |
| xຽວ | iaw | similar to the 'io' in 'Rio' |
| ແxວ | aew | combine ae and w |
| ເxວ | ehw | combine eh and w |
| ເxັວ | ew | same as ehw above, but shorter |
| ເxີຍ | oei | combine oe and i |
| xອຍ | awy | combine aw and y |

## consonants

Some Lao consonant sounds may be represented by two separate characters, just as 'ph' and 'f' are pronounced the same way in English.

| consonants | | |
|---|---|---|
| ສ, ຊ | s | as the 's' in 'soap' |
| ຝ, ຟ | f | same as the 'f' in 'fan' |
| ດ | d | as the 'd' in 'dodo' |
| ຕ | t | as the 't' in 'stop', similar to 'd' |
| ຖ, ທ | th | as the 't' as in 'tea' |
| ກ | k | as the 'k' in 'skin' |
| ຂ,ຄ | kh | as the 'k' in 'kite' |
| ບ | b | as the 'b' in 'boy' |
| ປ | p | as the 'p' in 'spin', similar to 'b' |
| ຜ, ພ | ph | as the 'p' in 'put' (but never as the 'ph' in 'phone') |
| ມ, ໝ | m | as the 'm' in 'man' |
| ນ, ໜ | n | as the 'n' in 'nun' |
| ງ | ng | as the 'ng' in 'sing' |
| ຍ | ny | similar to the 'ni' in 'onion' |
| ຈ | j | similar to the second 't' in 'stature' |
| ຢ | y | as the 'y' in 'yo-yo' |
| ລ, ຫຼ | l | as the 'l' in 'lick' |
| ວ | w | as the 'w' in 'wing' |
| ຫ, ຮ | h | as the 'h' in 'home' |

| play it again | |
|---|---|
| ໆ | this character denotes repetition of the previous word |

## variations in transliteration

In Laos you may come across many instances where the transliteration of vowels and consonants differs significantly, as in 'Louang' for Luang, 'Khouang' for Khuang or 'Xaignabouli' for Sainyabuli. The French spellings are particularly inconsistent in the use of the vowel 'ou', which in their transcriptions sometimes corresponds to a 'u' and sometimes to 'w'. An 'o' is often used for a short 'aw', as in 'Bo', which is pronounced more like baw.

Instances of 'v' in transcribed Lao words are generally pronounced more like a 'w'. For example, 'Vang Vieng' sounds more like Wang Wieng. In Vientiane, some of the older, educated upper class employ a strong 'v' rather than a 'w' sound.

Many standard place names in Roman script use an 'x' for what in English is 's'. There's no difference in pronunciation of the two; pronounce all instances of 'x' as 's'; for example, 'Xieng' should be pronounced sieng.

Finally, there's no 'r' sound in modern spoken Lao. When you see an 'r' in transcribed Lao, it's usually an old Lao or borrowed Thai transliteration; it should be pronounced like an 'l' in this case. Setthathirat (the name of a historic Lao king and common street name), for example, should actually be transcribed with an 'l' instead of an 'r' but usually isn't.

### wit & wisdom

The wise man is a good listener.

khón sá-làat nyáwm pẹn khón hûu-ják fang — ຄົນສະຫລາດຍອມ ເປັນຄົນຮູ້ຈັກຟັງ

ABOUT LAO

## tones

Traditionally, Lao is described as a monosyllabic, tonal language, like various forms of Thai and Chinese. Borrowed words from Sanskrit, Pali, French and English often have two or more syllables, however. Many syllables are differentiated by tone only. Consequently, the word sao, for example, can mean 'girl', 'morning', 'pillar' or 'twenty' depending on the tone. For people from non-tonal language backgrounds, this can take a bit of practice at first. Even when we 'know' the correct tone, our tendency to denote emotion, emphasis and questions through tone modulation often interferes with uttering the correct tone. So, the first rule in learning and using the tone system is to avoid overlaying your native intonation patterns onto Lao.

Vientiane Lao has six tones (compared with five in Standard Thai, four in Mandarin and up to nine in Cantonese). Three of the tones are level (low, mid and high) while three follow pitch inclines (rising, high falling and low falling). All six variations in pitch are relative to the speaker's natural vocal range, so that one person's low tone is not necessarily the same pitch as another person's. Hence, keen pitch recognition is not a prerequisite for learning a tonal language like Lao. A relative distinction between pitch contours is all that's necessary, just as it is with all languages (English and other European languages use intonation, too, just in a different way).

On a visual curve, the tones look like this:

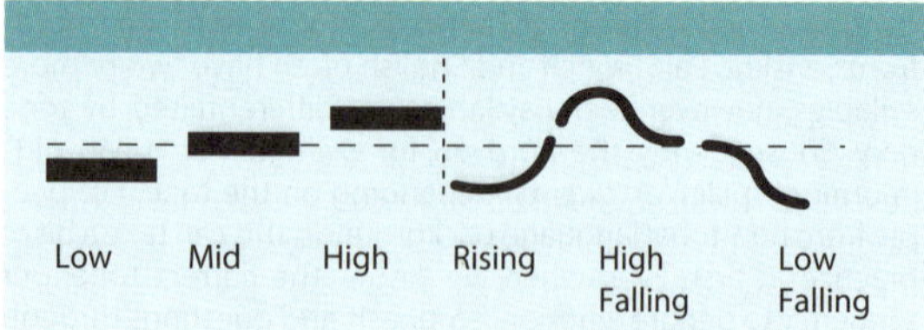


- The low tone is produced at the relative bottom of your conversational tonal range – usually flat and level (though not everyone pronounces it flat and level – some Vientiane natives add a slight rising tone to the end). For example, dịi (ດີ, good).
- The mid tone is flat like the low tone, but spoken at the relative middle of the speaker's vocal range. No tone mark is used. For example, het (ເຮັດ, do).
- The high tone is flat again, this time at the relative top of your vocal range. For example, héua (ເຮືອ, boat).
- The rising tone begins a bit below the mid tone and rises to just at or above the high tone. For example, sǎam (ສາມ, three).
- The high falling tone begins at or above the high tone and falls to the mid level. For example, sâo (ເຊົ້າ, morning).
- The low falling tone begins at about the mid level and falls to the level of the low tone. For example, khào (ເຂົ້າ, rice).

## script

This section will help those interested in learning about the fascinating, if somewhat complicated, Lao writing system. Fear not – if you're eager to hit the streets and speak Lao, skipping this section will not hinder your ability to communicate.

Prior to the consolidation of various Lao méuang (principalities) in the 14th century, there was little demand for a written language. When a written language was deemed necessary by the Lan Xang monarchy, Lao scholars based their script on an early alphabet devised by the Thais (which in turn had been created by Khmer scholars who used Mon scripts as models!). The alphabet used in Laos is closer to the original prototype; the original Thai script was later extensively revised (which is why Lao appears 'older' to orthographists than Thai, even though it's newer as a written language).

Before 1975, at least four spelling systems were in use. As modern printing never really established itself in Laos (most advanced textbooks being in Thai, French or Vietnamese before the revolution), Lao spelling wasn't standardised until after the Pathet Lao takeover. The current system has been highly simplified by omitting all literally transcribed spellings from foreign loan words. Instead of transliterating the Sanskrit nagara (city) letter for letter, for example, the new script uses only the letters actually pronounced in Lao, na-kháwn. Every letter written is pronounced, which means Lao script can be learned much more quickly than Thai or Khmer, both of which typically attempt to transcribe foreign borrowings letter for letter no matter what the actual pronunciation is.

Other scripts still in use include láo thám (dhamma Lao), used for writing Pali scriptures, and various Thai tribal scripts, the most popular and widespread being that of the Thai Neua (which has become standardised via Xishuangbanna, China).

The Lao script today consists of 28 consonants (but only 20 separate sounds) and 35 vowel and diphthong possibilities (16 separate symbols in varying combinations). In addition to the-consonant and vowel symbols are four tone marks, only two of which are commonly used to create the six different tones (in combination with all the other symbols).

Written Lao proceeds from left to right, though vowel-symbols may be written before, above, below, 'around' (before, above and after) or after consonants, depending on the sign. Although learning the alphabet is not difficult, the writing system itself is fairly complex, so unless you're planning a lengthy stay in Laos, it should perhaps be foregone in favour of learning to actually speak the language.

## how spelling determines Lao tones

Several features combine to encode the correct tone for each word or syllable in written Lao. To begin with, all Lao consonants are divided into three 'classes': high, mid and low, each of which follows its own set of tone rules. Once you've established which consonant class begins the syllable, you look for the absence or presence of a tone mark over the initial consonant. Modern written Lao has two tone marks: the mâi èhk ( ່ ) and the mâi thóh ( ້ ).

In standard Vientiane Lao, all syllables with a mâi èhk are spoken with the mid tone. Those with the mâi thóh are spoken with a low falling tone if they begin with a high-class consonant, or with a high falling tone if they begin with mid- or low-class consonants.

If there is no tone-mark over the syllable, then, in addition to knowing the consonant class, you must also take into consideration the length of the vowel and whether or not the word ends with that vowel or with a consonant. (This doesn't apply to tone-marked words, since they all end either with a vowel or with a nasal, ie, ng or n.)

Syllables with a stop final (p, t or k) combined with a long vowel take one set of tones (low falling for high- and mid-class consonants, high falling for low-class consonants), while those with short vowels take another (high tone for high- and mid-class consonants, mid tone for low-class consonants). In the case of short vowels without a final consonant, the tone is the same as for syllables with short vowels and stop finals.

For words of more than one syllable, each syllable has its own discrete tone, governed by the spelling of that syllable. Unlike Thai, there are no unwritten vowels in Lao, so the tone of one syllable never influences the following syllable – at least not in the written language.

The following charts show how these factors – consonant class, tone-mark, vowel length and syllable final – combine to encode the six tones in written Vientiane Lao. Although the system may seem rather complicated at first, once you've learned all the Lao characters, you can refer to these charts while learning to read and eventually internalise the Lao tone system.

Note that Lao dialects spoken in parts of Laos outside Vientiane Province follow their own tone rules. Also note that even the tone system for the Vientiane dialect is widely debated and true standardisation has yet to be achieved.

## the tonal system

| Class | NTMNSF | mâi èhk | mâi thóh | SFLV | SFSV/ SV |
|---|---|---|---|---|---|
| High | rising | mid | LF | LF | high |
| Mid | low | mid | HF | LF | high |
| Low | high | mid | HF | HF | mid |

## examples with transliteration

| Class | NTMNS | mâi èhk | mâi thóh | SFLV | SFSV/ SV |
|---|---|---|---|---|---|
| High | ຂາວ khǎo | ຂ່າວ khao | ເຂົ້າ khào | ຫຼອດ lâwt | ສິດ sót |
| Mid | ດີ dịi | ຕ່າງ taang | ເຈົ້າ jâo | ຈອກ jàwk | ເດັກ dék |
| Low | ເງິນ ngóen | ນັ່ງ nang | ແລ້ວ lâew | ເລືອດ lêuat | ທຸກ thuk |

## key

| | |
|---|---|
| **LF** | low falling |
| **HF** | high falling |
| **SFSV/SV** | stop final, short vowel; or short vowel, no final consonant |
| **SFLV** | stop final, long vowel |
| **NTMNS** | no tone mark, no stop final |

The following outline provides an introduction to the basics of Lao grammar – it is not a complete description, but it provides the tools to start building your own Lao sentences for those conversations that lead off the beaten track.

## word order

In general, word order in Lao is very significant. For example, dâi (ໄດ້) placed immediately before the verb marks past tense, while the same word appearing immediately after the verb means 'can'. Although the basic word order in Lao sentences is subject-verb-object, it's not uncommon to place the object first, for emphasis.

**I don't like that bowl.**
thùay nân khàwy baw mak — ຖ້ວຍນັ້ນຂ້ອຍບໍ່ມັກ
(lit: bowl that I no like)

## nouns

Nouns never vary. They do not change to indicate plurality, and they do not need articles like 'a' or 'the'. Once you've learned the word for something, it stays the same. The word wat (ວັດ, temple), for example, never changes, no matter how many wat you're speaking about.

Verbs of physical action can be made into nouns by adding kạan (ການ) before the verb. Verbs describing abstract action – as well as adjectives – use khwáam (ຄວາມ) to form nouns.

| | | |
|---|---|---|
| **to travel** | dọen tháang | ເດີນທາງ |
| **travel (n)** | kạan dọen tháang | ການເດີນທາງ |
| **to think** | khit | ຄິດ |
| **thought (n)** | khwáam khit | ຄວາມຄິດ |
| **good (adj)** | dịi | ດີ |
| **good (n)** | khwáam dịi | ຄວາມດີ |

## adjectives

Lao adjectives always follow the nouns they modify, except in the names of certain food dishes (eg, 'grilled chicken' is pîng kai, ປີ້ງໄກ່) where the adjective precedes the noun. They don't change in any way to 'agree' with the noun.

In Lao, you don't need to insert the verb 'to be' when describing something. Instead of saying 'the house is red' as we do in English, the Lao comes out as simply 'house red'.

| | | |
|---|---|---|
| **big house** | héuan nyai<br>(lit: house big) | ເຮືອນໃຫຍ່ |
| **delicious food** | kheuang kín sâep<br>(lit: food delicious) | ເຄື່ອງກິນແຊບ |
| **The room is small.** | hàwng nâwy<br>(lit: room small) | ຫ້ອງນ້ອຍ |

## comparatives

Basically any adjective in Lao can be used to make comparisons by adding kwaa (ກ່ວາ) to it.

| | | |
|---|---|---|
| **good** | dịi | ດີ |
| **better** | dịi-kwaa | ດີກ່ວາ |
| **cheap** | thèuk | ຖືກ |
| **cheaper** | thèuk-kwaa | ຖືກກ່ວາ |

## superlatives

Any adjective may be made superlative by adding thii-sút (ທີ່ສຸດ).

| | | |
|---|---|---|
| **delicious** | sâep | ແຊບ |
| **the most delicious** | sâep thii-sút | ແຊບທີ່ສຸດ |
| **big** | nyai | ໃຫຍ່ |
| **biggest** | nyai thii-sút | ໃຫຍ່ທີ່ສຸດ |

## equivalence

To express equivalence or sameness, use khéu káp (ຄືກັບ, the same as) or khéu kạn (ຄືກັນ, the same).

**That kind is the same as this kind.**
sá-nit nân khéu káp sá-nit nîi — ຊະນິດນັ້ນຄືກັບຊະນິດນີ້
(lit: kind that khéu káp kind this)

**Lao customs are not the same.**
pá-phéh-níi láo baw khéu kạn — ປະເພນີລາວບໍ່ຄືກັນ
(lit: custom Lao no khéu kạn)

## adverbs

Adjectives that can logically be used to modify action may function as adverbs in Lao. Usually this is indicated by doubling the adjective; this kind of adverb always follows the verb.

| | | |
|---|---|---|
| **slow** | sâa | ຊ້າ |
| **slow horse** | mâa sâa<br>(lit: horse slow) | ມ້າຊ້າ |
| **Drive slowly.** | kháp lot sâa-sâa<br>(lit: drive car slow-slow) | ຂັບລົດຊ້າໆ |

Certain words and phrases function only as adverbs and, depending on the word or phrase, may either precede the verb or come at the end of the sentence.

## adverbs before the verb

| | | |
|---|---|---|
| **ever** | khóei | ເຄີຍ |
| **never** | baw khóei | ບໍ່ເຄີຍ |
| **perhaps** | bạang thíi | ບາງທີ |
| **probably** | àat já | ອາດຈະ |
| **rarely** | hăa nyâak | ຫາຫຍາກ |
| **sometimes** | bạang theua | ບາງເທື່ອ |
| **usually** | pók-ká-tí | ປົກກະຕິ |
| **yet; not yet** | nyáng | ຍັງ |

## adverbs at the end of a sentence

| | | |
|---|---|---|
| also | khéu kạn | ຄືກັນ |
| always | lêuay lêuay | ເລື້ອຍໆ |
| immediately | thán thíi | ທັນທີ |
| often | lêuay | ເລື້ອຍ |
| only | thao-nân | ເທົ່ານັ້ນ |

## pronouns

## demonstrative pronouns

Demonstrative pronouns are the verbal equivalent of pointing.

| pronoun | with noun | as a question |
|---|---|---|
| this<br>nîi<br>ນີ້ | this plate<br>jạan nîi<br>ຈານນີ້<br>(lit: plate nîi) | What's this?<br>nîi maen nyǎng<br>ນີ້ແມ່ນຫຍັງ<br>(lit: nîi be what) |
| that<br>nân<br>ນັ້ນ | that plate<br>jạan nân<br>ຈານນັ້ນ<br>(lit: plate nân) | How much is that?<br>nân thao-dại<br>ນັ້ນເທົ່າໃດ<br>(lit: nân equal what) |
| these<br>lǎo nîi<br>ເຫຼົ່ານີ້ | these plates<br>jạan lǎo nîi<br>ຈານເຫຼົ່ານີ້<br>(lit: plate lǎo nîi) | What are these?<br>lǎo nîi maen nyǎng<br>ເຫຼົ່ານີ້ແມ່ນຫຍັງ<br>(lit: lǎo nîi be what) |
| those<br>lǎo nân<br>ເຫຼົ່ານັ້ນ | those plates<br>jạan lạo nân<br>ຈານເຫຼົ່ານັ້ນ<br>(lit: plate lǎo nân) | How much are those?<br>lǎo nân thao-dại<br>ເຫຼົ່ານັ້ນເທົ່າໃດ<br>(lit: lǎo nân equal what) |

## personal pronouns

Lao has 10 common personal pronouns. They aren't used as frequently as their English equivalents since Lao is a 'subject-weak' language in which the subject of a sentence is often omitted after the first reference. There's no distinction between subject and object pronouns (ie, 'I' and 'me').

### all purpose pronouns

The pronouns in this box will get you through your conversations, but as the opportunity arises, take the time to get to know some of the politer or more appropriate pronouns (some are given in the sections following) – they offer a little more insight into Lao culture..

| | | |
|---|---|---|
| I/me | khàwy | ຂ້ອຍ |
| he/she | khǎo | ເຂົາ |
| it | mán | ມັນ |
| you (sg) | jâo | ເຈົ້າ |
| you (pl) | phûak jâo | ພວກເຈົ້າ |
| we | phûak háo | ພວກເຮົາ |
| us | phûak khàwy | ພວກຂ້ອຍ |
| they | phûak khǎo | ພວກເຂົາ |

## first person – i/we

**I/me (to most people)**
khàwy ຂ້ອຍ

**I/me (when speaking to elders or people with high status)**
kháa-nâwy ຂ້ານ້ອຍ

**we/us**
phûak háo; phûak khàwy ພວກເຮົາ/ພວກຂ້ອຍ
(lit: group we; group us)

## second person – you

| | | |
|---|---|---|
| you (sg) | **jâo** | ເຈົ້າ |
| you (pl) | **phûak jâo** (lit: group you) | ພວກເຈົ້າ |

The general all-purpose 'you' is **jâo**.

The pronoun **thaan** (ທ່ານ) is reserved for people in high social positions such as monks or government officials. You may also use it with Lao who are substantially older than you to show respect, although **jâo** is sufficient.

### other terms of address

Other terms of address you may hear, but probably won't use, include:

| | | |
|---|---|---|
| **lúng** | ລຸງ | **to an older man** (lit: uncle) |
| **pâa** | ປ້າ | **to an older woman** (lit: aunt) |
| **tọh** | ໂຕ | **to a lover or other intimate relation** |
| **êuay** | ເອື້ອຍ | **to a female or social equal** (lit: older sister) |
| **âai** | ອ້າຍ | **to a male or social equal** (lit: older brother) |
| **nâwng** | ນ້ອງ | **to someone of any gender younger than you** (lit: younger sibling) |

None of these kinship terms is appropriate for use by a foreigner with an elementary command of Lao.

## third person – he/she/it/they

**he/she (when speaking of most people)**
khăo ເຂົາ

**he/she (when speaking of elders or monks)**
phoen ເພິ່ນ

**he/she (when speaking about people you know)**
láo ລາວ

**he/she (when speaking about persons with high status)**
thaan ທ່ານ

**it (inanimate objects and animals)**
mán ມັນ

**they**
phûak added before khăo, láo ພວກ
or phoen as with 'you' (plural)

In general, khăo is the all-encompassing term; there is no gender or number distinction. When speaking of people you know personally, láo can be used, though for elders phoen is better.

For monks phoen should be substituted (same as for second-person) to express respect. For example:

**How many months has he been a monk?**

phoen bùat pẹn khúu-bạa ເພິ່ນບວດເປັນຄູບາໄດ້
dâi ják dẹuan lâew ຈັກເດືອນແລ້ວ

(lit: phoen ordain be monk how many month already)

## possession

Khǎwng (ຂອງ) is used to denote possession and is roughly equivalent to the preposition 'of' or the verb 'belongs to' in English.

**my bag**
thǒng khǎwng khàwy — ຖົງຂອງຂ້ອຍ
(lit: bag khǎwng I)

**his/her seat**
bawn nang khǎwng láo — ບ່ອນນັ່ງຂອງລາວ
(lit: place sit khǎwng he/she)

**Does this belong to you?**
nîi máen khǎwng jâo baw — ນີ້ແມ່ນຂອງເຈົ້າບໍ່
(lit: this be khǎwng you no)

The ever-versatile khǎwng can also be used as a noun to mean 'stuff' or 'things'.

**She went to buy some things.**
khǎo pai sêu kheuang khǎwng — ເຂົາໄປຊື້ເຄື່ອງຂອງ
(lit: she go buy some khǎwng)

For 'whose' use khǎwng phǎi (ຂອງໃຜ, belong who).

**Whose plate is this?**
jąan nîi maen khǎwng phǎi — ຈານນີ້ແມ່ນຂອງໃຜ
(lit: plate this be khäwng phäi)

## verbs

### tense

Lao verbs do not change their spellings or pronunciations to account for time references. Time is conveyed by context and by means of adding time indicators like 'today', 'tomorrow', 'yesterday', 'last year'and so on, or by adding markers that indicate ongoing action, completed action and to-be-completed action.

Out of context, without a time reference, the sentence láo kịn kai (ລາວກິນໄກ່) could mean 'She/He eats/ate/has eaten/will eat chicken'.

Adding mêu-wáan-nîi (ມື້ວານນີ້, yesterday) to the sentence, as in mêu-wáan-nîi láo kịn kai (ມື້ວານນີ້ລາວກິນໄກ່), gives this sentence a definite 'past' sense. Likewise mêu-nîi (ມື້ນີ້, today) láo kịn kai gives it a 'present' sense.

As in English, the time sense can be further qualified by the addition of words like 'often', 'seldom', 'every day', etc.

## ongoing action

Verbs used in the absence of time markers such as 'yesterday' and 'tomorrow', are usually taken to indicate present or ongoing action.

**They are playing guitar.**
phûak khǎo lìn kịi-tạa ພວກເຂົາຫລິ້ນກີຕາ
(lit: group he/she play guitar)

### wit & wisdom

**If you are shy with the teacher you won't learn; if you are shy with women you won't get married.**

ạai khúu baw dâi khwáam hûu ạai sûu baw dâi mía ອາຍຄູບໍ່ໄດ້ຄວາມຮູ້ ອາຍຊູ້ບໍ່ໄດ້ເມຍ

## completed action

The most common way of expressing completed action in Lao is by adding the past tense word lâew (ແລ້ວ) after the verb (if there is no direct or indirect object; after the object otherwise).

**We went to Vientiane.**
phûak khàwy pại wíeng jạn lâew ພວກເຮົາໄປວຽງຈັນແລ້ວ
(lit: group I go Vientiane lâew)

grammar

**I spent the money.**

khàwy jai ngóen lâew — ຂ້ອຍຈ່າຍເງິນແລ້ວ

(lit: I spend money lâew)

Note that, as in the last example above, lâew can refer to a current condition that began in the immediate past.

Dâi (ໄດ້, to be able) also shows past tense but, unlike lâew, it's never used with present action. It immediately precedes the verb, and is often used in conjunction with lâew. It is more commonly employed in negative statements than in the affirmative.

**Our friends didn't go to Luang Prabang.**

pheuan phûak háo baw dâi pại lǔang pha-bạng — ເພື່ອນພວກເຮົາບໍ່ໄດ້ໄປຫລວງພະບາງ

(lit: friend group we no dâi go Luang Prabang)

## to-be-completed action

The future markers já (ຈະ) or sii (ຊິ) are used to mark an action to be completed in the future. It always appears directly before the verb.

**She/He will buy rice.**

láo já sêu khào — ລາວຈະຊື້ເຂົ້າ

(lit: she/he já buy rice)

## making requests & giving commands

Khǎw (ຂໍ), a word that cannot be directly translated into English, is used to make polite requests. Depending on the context, it's roughly equivalent to 'please give me' or 'may I ask for'. Khǎw always comes at the beginning of a sentence, and is often used in conjunction with the added 'politener' dae (ແດ່) – spoken at the end of the sentence.

**Please pass some rice.**

khǎw khào dae — ຂໍເຂົ້າແດ່

(lit: khǎw rice dae)

If you want someone to do something, you can politely preface the sentence with khǎw suay (ຂໍຊ່ວຍ, 'May I ask help?') or sóen (ເຊີນ, 'I invite you'). In English the closest equivalent is 'please'.

**Please close the window.**
khǎw suay pít pawng îam dae ຂໍຊ່ວຍປິດປ່ອງອ້ຽມແດ່
(lit: khǎw suay help close window dae)

**Please sit down.**
sóen nang ເຊີນນັ່ງ
(lit: sóen sit)

To express a greater sense of urgency, use dòe (ເດີ້) at the end of a sentence.

**Close the door.**
pít pá-tųu dòe ປິດປະຕູເດີ້
(lit: close door dòe)

## to be

The verb 'to be' in Lao is much more limited in function than its English counterpart. There are two forms – maen (ແມ່ນ) and pęn (ເປັນ) – which are only used to join nouns and/or pronouns. They are not used to join nouns or pronouns with adjectives (see Adjectives, page 22).

As a rule, use maen for objects and pęn for people.

**This is a pedicab.**
ąn-nîi maen sǎam-lâw ອັນນີ້ແມ່ນສາມລໍ້
(lit: this maen pedicab)

**I'm a musician.**
khàwy pœn nak-d§n-t¤i ຂ້ອຍເປັນນັກດົນຕີ
(lit: I pęn musician)

Pęn is also used to show ability (see Can, page 35) and and can as well mean 'to have' when describing a person's condition (see To Have, page 32).

If you want to say 'there is ...' or 'there are ...', the verb míi (ມີ, 'to have') is used instead of pẹn. Míi here means 'to have' in the sense of 'to exist' – you're likely to hear it in sentences like:

**In Vientiane, there are many cars.**
yuu wiéng jạn míi lot lǎai — ຢູ່ວຽງຈັນມີລົດຫລາຍ
(lit: stay Vientiane míi car many)

**There's a large Buddha image at Wat Ong Teu.**
wat ọng têu míi pha-phut-tha-hûup nyai — ວັດອົງຕື້ມີ ພະພຸດທະຮູບໃຫຍ່
(lit: Wat Ong Teu míi Buddha-image big)

## to have

Míi (ມີ) means 'to have' and can also be used to mean 'there is' or 'there are'.

**I have a bicycle.**
khàwy míi lot thìip — ຂ້ອຍມີລົດຖີບ
(lit: I míi vehicle pedal)

**Do you have fried rice noodles?**
míi phát fŏe baw — ມີພັດເຝີບໍ່
(lit: míi fry rice-noodle no)

Pẹn, 'to be', is used in the sense of 'to have' when describing a person's condition.

**I have a fever.**
khàwy pen khài — ຂ້ອຍເປັນໄຂ້
(lit: I pẹn fever)

**She/He has a cold.**
láo pẹn wát — ລາວເປັນຫວັດ
(lit: she/he pẹn common-cold)

**grammar doesn't rule!**

Grammar rules are certainly made to be broken – don't be afraid to experiment with some of the phrases and formulas you find in this section. Communicate in any way you can, string words together and don't hesitate to create a few 'interesting' sentences! The finer points will come ...

## negatives

Baw (ບໍ່, no) is the main negative marker in Lao. Nyáng (ຍັງ) is also used to mean 'not yet' in answer to questions that end in lâew baw (ແລ້ວບໍ່, see Questions, page 36). Nyáng is placed before baw in a complete sentence, or alone to mean simply 'Not yet'.

Any verb or adjective may be negated by the insertion of baw immediately before it.

**She/He isn't thirsty.**
láo baw yàak nâm — ລາວບໍ່ຢາກນ້ຳ
(lit: she/he baw want water)

**I don't have any cash.**
khàwy baw mí ngóen — ຂ້ອຍບໍ່ມີເງິນ
(lit: I baw have money)

**We're not French.**
phûak háo baw pẹn khón fa-lang — ພວກເຮົາບໍ່ເປັນຄົນຝະລັ່ງ
(lit: group we baw be people French)

**John has never gone to Savannaket.**
john baw khóei pại sa-wăn-na-khèt — ຈອນບໍ່ເຄີຍໄປ ສະຫວັນນະເຂດ
(lit: John baw ever go Savannaket)

**We won't go to Pakse tomorrow.**
mêu eun phûak háo baw pại pàak-séh — ມື້ອື່ນພວກເຮົາ ບໍ່ໄປປາກເຊ
(lit: day other group we baw go Pakse)

**You haven't eaten yet.**
jâo nyáng baw thán kịn khào — ເຈົ້າຍັງບໍ່ທັນກິນເຂົ້າ
(lit: you nyáng baw yet eat rice)

## modals

Like most other languages, Lao makes use of words like 'should', 'want to', 'need to' or 'can' in conjunction with verbs to express obligation, want/need and ability (eg, must do, need to do, can do').

### obligation

Khúan (ຄວນ) serves as 'should' or 'ought to', usually in conjunction with jà, the marker for to-be-completed action.

**You should eat.**
jâo khúan já kịn khào — ເຈົ້າຄວນຈະກິນເຂົ້າ
(lit: you khúan já eat rice)

**She/He shouldn't do that.**
láo baw khúan hét naew nân — ລາວບໍ່ຄວນເຮັດແນວນັ້ນ
(lit: she/he no khúan do like that)

### want

Yàak (ຢາກ) is placed in front of the verb to express 'want' or 'desire'.

**The dog wants to eat.**
mǎa yàak kịn khào — ໝາຢາກກິນເຂົ້າ
(lit: dog yàak eat rice)

**I don't want to walk.**
khàwy baw yàak nyaang — ຂ້ອຍບໍ່ຢາກຍ່າງ
(lit: I no yàak walk)

When 'want' is used with a noun, it takes the form of either ạo (ເອົາ, take) or yàak dâi (ຢາກໄດ້, want to get).

**I want bananas.**
khàwy ạo kûay — ຂ້ອຍເອົາກ້ວຍ
(lit: I ạo banana)

**Tom wants a shirt.**
thawm yàak dâi sèua — ທອມຢາກໄດ້ເສື້ອ
(lit: Tom yàak dâi shirt)

## need

The word tâwng (ຕ້ອງ) comes before verbs to mean 'must' or 'need to'. When using 'need' plus a noun, use tâwng-kạan (ຕ້ອງການ).

**I must go to the market.**
khàwy tâwng pại tá-làat — ຂ້ອຍຕ້ອງໄປຕະຫລາດ
(lit: I tâwng go market)

**We need to look for a house.**
háo tâwng hǎa héuan — ເຮົາຕ້ອງຫາເຮືອນ
(lit: we tâwng seek house)

**You don't have to stay here.**
jâo baw tâwng phák yuu-nîi — ເຈົ້າບໍ່ຕ້ອງພັກຢູ່ນີ້
(lit: you no tâwng stay here)

**I need a bicycle.**
khàwy tâwng-kạan lot-thìip — ຂ້ອຍຕ້ອງການລົດຖີບ
(lit: I tâwng-kạan bicycle)

## can

Lao has three ways of expressing 'can': dâi, pẹn and sǎa-màat. Dâi (ໄດ້) means 'to be able to' or 'to be allowed to' and is the more general equivalent of the English 'can'. It always follows the verb (and negative marker and object, if any).

**Can you go?**
pại dâi baw — ໄປໄດ້ບໍ່
(lit: go dâi no)

**I can't go.**

pại baw dâi — ໄປບໍ່ໄດ້

(lit: go no dâi)

**I can't eat pork.**

kịn sîin mŭu baw dâi — ກິນຊີ້ນໝູບໍ່ໄດ້

(lit: eat piece pig no dâi)

Pẹn (ເປັນ) may mean 'can' in the sense of 'to know how to'. Like dâi, it ends the verb phrase.

**She/He knows how to play guitar.**

láo lìn kịi-tạa pẹn — ລາວຫລິ້ນກີຕາເປັນ

(lit: she/he play guitar pẹn)

Săa-màat (ສາມາດ) is used as 'can' to express physical possibility or ability. Unlike dâi and pẹn, it's placed before the verb.

**I can't lift that.**

khàwy baw săa-màat nyok an-nân kèun — ຂ້ອຍບໍ່ສາມາດຍົກອັນນັ້ນຂຶ້ນ

(lit: I no săa-màat lift classifier-that up)

## questions

Lao has two ways of forming questions: use of a question word like 'who', 'how', 'what', etc or through the addition of a tag like 'isn't it?' or 'no?' to the end of the sentence.

Many English-speakers instinctively place an English question inflection to the end of a Lao question; try to avoid doing this as it will usually throw off the Lao tones.

### question words

Note the placement of Lao question words in a sentence. Some come at the beginning of the question, others at the end.

**What?**

nyăng — ຫຍັງ

What do you need?
jâo tawng-kạan nyǎng — ເຈົ້າຕ້ອງການຫຍັງ
(lit: you need nyǎng)

How?
náew-dại — ແນວໃດ
(lit: manner which)

How do you do it?
hét náew-dại — ເຮັດແນວໃດ
(lit: do náew-dại)

Who?
phǎi — ໃຜ

Who's sitting there?
phǎi nang yuu hân — ໃຜນັ່ງຢູ່ຫັ້ນ
(lit: phǎi sit stay there)

When?
wéh-láa dại — ເວລາໃດ
(lit: time which)

When will you go to Luang Prabang?
wéh-láa dại já pại lǔang pha-bạng — ເວລາໃດຈະໄປ ຫລວງພະບາງ
(lit: wéh-láa dại future-marker go Luang Prabang)

Why?
pẹn nyǎng — ເປັນຫຍັງ
(lit: be what)

Why are you so quiet?
pẹn nyǎng jâo mit thâe — ເປັນຫຍັງເຈົ້າມິດແທ້
(lit: pẹn nyǎng you quiet real)

How much?
thâo dại — ເທົ່າໃດ
(lit: equal what)

grammar

**How much is this?**
nîi thao dại — ນີ້ເທົ່າໃດ
(lit: this thâo dại)

**Where?**
yuu sǎi — ຢູ່ໃສ
(lit: stay where)

**Where's the bathroom?**
hàwng nâam yuu sǎi — ຫ້ອງນ້ຳຢູ່ໃສ
(lit: room water yuu sǎi)

**Which?**
ạn dại — ອັນໃດ
(lit: classifier which)

**Which one do you like?**
jâo mak ạn dại — ເຈົ້າມັກອັນໃດ
(lit: you like ạn dại)

## tags

Just like in English, a 'tag' comes at the end of a sentence and requests confirmation of what has been proposed in that same sentence.

**isn't it?/is it?**
baw — ບໍ່

**The weather's hot, isn't it?**
ạa-kàat hâwn baw — ອາກາດຮ້ອນບໍ່
(lit: air hot baw)

**right?**
maen baw — ແມ່ນບໍ່

**You're a writer, right?**
jâo pẹn nak-khían maen baw — ເຈົ້າເປັນນັກຂຽນແມ່ນບໍ່
(lit: you be student maen baw)

**or not?**
lěu baw — ຫລືບໍ່

**Do you want to go out or not?**
yàak pại lìn lěu baw — ຢາກໄປຫລິ້ນຫລືບໍ່
(lit: want go play lěu baw)

**yet?**
lâew baw — ແລ້ວບໍ່

**Have you eaten yet?**
jâo kịn khào lâew baw — ເຈົ້າກິນເຂົ້າແລ້ວບໍ່
(lit: you eat rice lâew baw)

**eh?**
lěu — ຫລື

## answers

To answer questions in Lao, you merely repeat the verb, with or without the negative particle baw (ບໍ່). Informally, a negative particle will do for a negative reply.

| | | |
|---|---|---|
| **Do you want to drink tea?** | yàak kịn nâm sáa baw<br>(lit: want eat water tea no) | ຢາກກິນນ້ຳຊາບໍ່ |
| **Yes.** | yàak kịn<br>(lit: want eat) | ຢາກກິນ |
| **No.** | baw yàak kin<br>(lit: no want eat) | ບໍ່ຢາກກິນ |
| **Are you well?** | sá-bạai-dịi baw<br>(lit: well no) | ສະບາຍດີບໍ່ |
| **Yes.** | sá-bạai-dịi<br>(lit: well) | ສະບາຍດີ |
| **No.** | baw sá-bạai<br>(lit: no well) | ບໍ່ສະບາຍ |
| **Have you eaten yet?** | kịn khào lâew baw<br>(lit: eat rice already no) | ກິນເຂົ້າແລ້ວບໍ່ |
| **Yes.** | kịn lâew<br>(lit: eat already) | ກິນແລ້ວ |

| | | |
|---|---|---|
| No. | nyáng (lit: yet) | ຍັງ |
| You're a teacher, aren't you? | jâo pẹn khúu maen baw (lit: you be teacher be no) | ເຈົ້າເປັນຄູແມ່ນບໍ່ |
| Yes. | maen (lit: be) | ແມ່ນ |
| No. | baw maen (lit: no be) | ບໍ່ແມ່ນ |
| Are you happy? | dịi-jại lĕu baw (lit: happy or no) | ດີໃຈຫລືບໍ່ |
| Yes. | dịi-jại (lit: happy) | ດີໃຈ |
| No. | baw (lit: no) | ບໍ່ |

## classifiers

Classifiers or counters are words which define the category that an item being counted belongs to. These are comparable to words like 'slice' and 'sheet' in English (as in 'two slices of bread' or 'three sheets of paper').

To state a quantity of something in Lao, you first name the thing you want, then the number and finally the classifier or counter of the item – so five oranges is màak-kîang hàa nuay (ໝາກກ້ຽງຫ້າໜ່ວຍ, orange five classifier). Every noun that's countable in Lao takes a classifier.

### common classifiers

| | | |
|---|---|---|
| animals, furniture, clothing | tọh | ໂຕ |
| candles, books | hŭa | ຫົວ |
| Buddha images | ọng | ອົງ |
| buses, cars, bikes, vehicles | khán | ຄັນ |

| | | |
|---|---|---|
| fruit, balls | nuay | ໜ່ວຍ |
| glasses (of water, tea, etc) | jàwk | ຈອກ |
| houses | lǎng | ຫລັງ |
| letters, newspapers (flatsheets) | sá-báp | ສະບັບ |
| monks | hùup | ຮູບ |
| pairs of items (people, things) | khuu | ຄູ່ |
| people | khón | ຄົນ |
| pills, seeds, small gems | kaen | ແກ່ນ |
| plates (food) | jạan | ຈານ |
| rolls (toilet paper, film) | mûan | ມ້ວນ |
| round hollow objects, leaves | bại | ໃບ |
| sets of things | sut | ຊຸດ |
| slices (cakes, cloth) | phaen | ແຜ່ນ |
| small objects, miscellaneous | tọh | ໂຕ |

If you don't know (or forget) the appropriate classifier, tọh (ໂຕ) may be used for almost any small thing. Alternatively, the Lao sometimes repeat the noun rather than not use a classifier at all.

## prepositions

| | | |
|---|---|---|
| above | tháang thóeng | ທາງເທິງ |
| across from | khâam káp | ຂ້າມກັບ |
| adjacent to | yuu khàang káp | ຢູ່ຂ້າງກັບ |
| around | hâwp | ຮອບ |
| at | yuu | ຢູ່ |
| behind | tháang lǎng | ທາງຫລັງ |
| beside | tháang khàang | ທາງຂ້າງ |
| from | tae | ແຕ່ |
| in (and inside) | nái | ໃນ |
| in front of | tháang nàa | ທາງໜ້າ |
| of | khǎwng | ຂອງ |
| on | thóeng | ເທິງ |
| opposite | kọng kạn khâam káp | ກົງກັນຂ້າມກັບ |
| under | kàwng | ກ້ອງ |
| with | káp/nám | ກັບ/ນຳ |

## conjunctions

| | | |
|---|---|---|
| and | lae | ແລະ |
| because | phaw waa | ເພາະວ່າ |
| but | tae waa | ແຕ່ວ່າ |
| or | lěu waa | ຫຼືວ່າ |
| since | tâng tae | ຕັ້ງແຕ່ |
| so (therefore) | phaw sá-nân | ເພາະສະນັ້ນ |
| so that (in order to) | pheua | ເພື່ອ |
| then | lâew | ແລ້ວ |
| when | mêua/wéh-láa | ເມື່ອ/ເວລາ |

ABOUT LAO

See Classifiers, p40, for important information on how to use 'classifiers' or 'counters' with Lao numbers.

## cardinal numbers

ເລກນັບ

| | | |
|---|---|---|
| zero | sǔun | ສູນ |
| one | neung | ໜຶ່ງ |
| two | sǎwng | ສອງ |
| three | sǎam | ສາມ |
| four | sii | ສີ່ |
| five | hàa | ຫ້າ |
| six | hók | ຫົກ |
| seven | jét | ເຈັດ |
| eight | paet | ແປດ |
| nine | kâo | ເກົ້າ |
| 10 | síp | ສິບ |
| 11 | síp-ét | ສິບເອັດ |
| 12 | síp-sǎwng | ສິບສອງ |
| 13 | síp-sǎam | ສິບສາມ |
| 14 | síp-sii | ສິບສີ່ |
| ...-teen | síp-... | ສິບ ... |
| 20 | sáo | ຊາວ |
| 21 | sáo-ét | ຊາວເອັດ |
| 22 | sáo-sǎwng | ຊາວສອງ |
| 23 | sáo-sǎam | ຊາວສາມ |
| 30 | sǎam-síp | ສາມສິບ |
| 40 | sii-síp | ສີ່ສິບ |
| 50 | hàa-síp | ຫ້າສິບ |

| | | |
|---|---|---|
| 60 | hók-síp | ຫົກສິບ |
| 70 | jét-síp | ເຈັດສິບ |
| 80 | pàet-síp | ແປດສິບ |
| 90 | kâo-síp | ເກົ້າສິບ |
| 100 | hâwy | ຮ້ອຍ |
| 200 | sǎwng hâwy | ສອງຮ້ອຍ |
| 300 | sǎam hâwy | ສາມຮ້ອຍ |
| 1000 | phán | ພັນ |
| 10,000 | meun (síp-phán) | ໝື່ນ (ສິບພັນ) |
| 100,000 | sǎen (hâwy phán) | ແສນ (ຮ້ອຍພັນ) |
| million | lâan | ລ້ານ |
| billion | têu (phan láan) | ຕື້ |

## ordinal numbers

ເລກລຳດັບ

These are formed by adding thíi (ທີ່) before the cardinal numbers.

| | | |
|---|---|---|
| first | thíi neung | ທີ່ໜຶ່ງ |
| second | thíi sǎwng | ທີ່ສອງ |
| thirty-first | thíi sǎam-síp-ét | ທີສາມສິບເອັດ |

BASICS

## fractions

ເລກສ່ວນ

Fractions are formed by inserting suan (ສ່ວນ, part) before the lower integer. 'Half' has its own term, khoeng (ເຄິ່ງ).

| | | |
|---|---|---|
| **one quarter (1/4)** | neung suan sii | ໜຶ່ງສ່ວນສີ່ |
| **one eighth (1/8)** | neung suan pàet | ໜຶ່ງສ່ວນແປດ |
| **three eighths (3/8)** | săam suan pàet | ສາມສ່ວນແປດ |
| **half (1/2)** | khoeng | ເຄິ່ງ |

## useful words

ບາງຄຳສັບທີ່ເປັນປະໂຫຍດ

| | | |
|---|---|---|
| **count** | nap | ນັບ |
| **couple/pair** | khuu | ຄູ່ |
| **decimal point** | jút | ຈຸດ |
| **dozen** | lŏh | ໂຫຼ |
| **equal (adj)** | thao kạn | ເທົ່າກັນ |
| **equal to** | thao káp | ເທົ່າກັບ |
| **large** | nyai | ໃຫຍ່ |
| **least** | nâwy thii-sút | ນ້ອຍທີ່ສຸດ |
| **little/few** | nâwy | ນ້ອຍ |
| **many** | lăai | ຫລາຍ |

numbers & amounts

| | | |
|---|---|---|
| minus | lop | ລົບ |
| most | lǎai thii-sút | ຫລາຍທີ່ສຸດ |
| much | lǎai | ຫລາຍ |
| number (amount) | jạm-núan | ຈຳນວນ |
| number (numeral) | nâm-bọe (lêhk) | ນຳເບີ້(ເລກ) |
| plus | pá-sǒm/buak | ປະສົມ/ບວກ |
| small | nâwy | ນ້ອຍ |
| weight | nâm-nak | ນ້ຳໜັກ |

BASICS

## time

ເວລາ

The Lao tell time using a 12-hour system that divides the day into four sections (ຕອນ, tąwn). The 'dead of night' period (11 pm to 6 am) is known as kąang khéun (ກາງຄືນ).

| | | |
|---|---|---|
| **6 am to noon** | tąwn sâo | ຕອນເຊົ້າ |
| **noon to 3 or 4 pm** | tąwn baai | ຕອນບ່າຍ |
| **3 or 4 pm to 6 pm** | tąwn láeng | ຕອນແລງ |
| **6 to 11 pm** | tąwn khám | ຕອນຄ່ຳ |

Clock time is expressed in móhng (ໂມງ, hour) and náa-thíi (ນາທີ, minutes), plus one of the above times of day. When speaking, baai (ບ່າຍ, afternoon) comes before the hour; all the other times of day come after.

| | | |
|---|---|---|
| **What time is it?** | wéh-láa ják móhng | ເວລາຈັກໂມງ |
| **9 am** | kâo móhng sâo | ເກົ້າໂມງເຊົ້າ |
| **midday** | thiang | ທ່ຽງ |
| **1 pm** | baai móhng | ບ່າຍໂມງ |
| **2.15 pm** | baai sǎwng móhng síp-hàa | ບ່າຍສອງໂມງສິບຫ້າ |
| **5 pm** | hàa móhng láeng | ຫ້າໂມງແລງ |
| **8.20 pm** | pàet móhng sáo tąwn khám | ແປດໂມງຊາວຕອນຄ່ຳ |
| **midnight** | thiang khéun | ທ່ຽງຄືນ |

When expressing time in terms of number of hours, use sua-móhng (ຊົ່ວໂມງ) rather than móhng.

| | | |
|---|---|---|
| **three hours** | sǎam sua-móhng | ສາມຊົ່ວໂມງ |

## days of the week

ວັນໃນສັບປະດາ

| | | |
|---|---|---|
| Sunday | wán ạa-thit | ວັນອາທິດ |
| Monday | wán jạn | ວັນຈັນ |
| Tuesday | wán ạng-kháan | ວັນອັງຄານ |
| Wednesday | wán phut | ວັນພຸດ |
| Thursday | wán pha-hát | ວັນພະຫັດ |
| Friday | wán súk | ວັນສຸກ |
| Saturday | wán sǎo | ວັນເສົາ |
| week | ạa-thit | ອາທິດ |
| weekend | sǎo-ạa-thit | ເສົາອາທິດ |

## months

ເດືອນ

| | | |
|---|---|---|
| January | dẹuan máng-kạwn | ເດືອນມັງກອນ |
| February | dẹuan kụm-pháa | ເດືອນກຸມພາ |
| March | dẹuan mi-náa | ເດືອນມີນາ |
| April | dẹuan méh-sǎa | ເດືອນເມສາ |
| May | dẹuan pheut-sá-pháa | ເດືອນພຶດສະພາ |
| June | dẹuan mi-thú-náa | ເດືອນມິຖຸນາ |
| July | dẹuan kạw-la-kót | ເດືອນກໍລະກົດ |
| August | dẹuan sǐng-hǎa | ເດືອນສິງຫາ |
| September | dẹuan kạn-yáa | ເດືອນກັນຍາ |
| October | dẹuan tú-láa | ເດືອນຕຸລາ |
| November | dẹuan pha-jík | ເດືອນພະຈິກ |
| December | dẹuan than-wáa | ເດືອນທັນວາ |
| month | dẹuan | ເດືອນ |
| half a month | khoeng dẹuan | ເຄິງເດືອນ |
| a month and a half | dẹuan khoeng | ເດືອນເຄິງ |

## seasons

ລະດູ

**hot season; dry season (Mar-May)**
la-dụu hâwn; la-dụu lâeng — ລະດູຮ້ອນ/ລະດູແລ້ງ
**rainy season (Jun-Oct)**
la-dụu fŏn — ລະດູຝົນ
**cool season (Nov-Feb)**
la-dụu năo — ລະດູໜາວ

## dates

ວັນທີ່

The traditional Lao calendar, like the calendars of China, Vietnam, Cambodia and Thailand, is a solar-lunar mix. The year itself is reckoned by solar phases, while the months are divided according to lunar phases (unlike the Gregorian calendar in which months as well as years are reckoned by the sun). The Lao Buddhist Era (BE) calendar figures year one as 543 BC, which means that you must subtract 543 from the Lao calendar year to arrive at the 'Christian era' (Gregorian) calendar familiar in the West (eg, AD 2001 is 2544 BE according to the Lao Buddhist calendar).

Most educated Lao are also familiar with the 'Christian era' (khit sák-á-lâat) calendar.

**2544 (BE)**
(pháw sǎw) sǎwng phán hàa hâwy sii-síp sii — ສອງພັນຫ້າຮ້ອຍສີ່ສິບສີ່
**2001 (AD)**
(kháw sǎw) sǎwng phán neung — ສອງພັນໜຶ່ງ

Days of the month are numbered according to the familiar Gregorian calendar.

**13th January**
wán thíi síp-săam dẹuan máng-kạwn — ວັນທີສິບສາມເດືອນມັງກອນ

**date**
wán thíi — ວັນທີ່
**year**
pịi — ປີ
**What date?**
wán thíi thao-dại? — ວັນທີ່ເທົ່າໃດ

## present

ປະຈຸບັນ

| | | |
|---|---|---|
| today | mêu nîi | ມື້ນີ້ |
| this evening | láeng nîi | ແລງນີ້ |
| tonight | khéun nîi | ຄືນນີ້ |
| this morning | sâo nîi | ເຊົ້ານີ້ |
| this afternoon | baai nîi | ບ່າຍນີ້ |
| this month | dẹuan nîi | ເດືອນນີ້ |
| all day long | ta-làwt mêu | ຕະຫລອດມື້ |

## past

ອາດີດ

| | | |
|---|---|---|
| yesterday | mêu wáan nîi | ມື້ວານນີ້ |
| the day before yesterday | mêu séun | ມື້ຊືນ |
| last week | ạa-thit lâew | ອາທິດແລ້ວ |
| two weeks ago | sǎwng ạa-thit lâew | ສອງອາທິດແລ້ວ |
| three months ago | sǎam dẹuan lâew | ສາມເດືອນແລ້ວ |
| four years ago | kawn nîi sii pịi | ກ່ອນນີ້ສີ່ປີ |

### tense tones

You don't need to worry about speaking in the right tense to speak Lao grammatically, but if you want to be understood, remember that Lao is a tonal language – so always be aware that you have to avoid English intonation, such as raising your voice at the end of a question (see page 36 for more help with this).

# future

ອະນາຄົດ

| | | |
|---|---|---|
| **tomorrow** | mêu eun | ມື້ອື່ນ |
| **the day after tomorrow** | mêu héu | ມື້ຮື |
| **next week** | ąa-thit nàa | ອາທິດໜ້າ |
| **next month** | dęuan nàa | ເດືອນໜ້າ |
| **two more months** | ìik sǎwng dęuan | ອີກສອງເດືອນ |

# festivals & national holidays

ເທດສະການທາງການແລະວັນພັກ

Festivals in Laos are mostly linked to agricultural seasons or historical Buddhist holidays. The general word for festival in Lao is bųn (ບຸນ, often written as boun). Exact dates for festivals may vary from year to year, either because of the lunar calendar – which isn't quite in sync with the Gregorian solar calendar – or because local authorities decide to change festival dates.

On dates noted as public holidays, all government offices and banks will be closed.

## february

| | | |
|---|---|---|
| **Magha Puja** | ma-khà bųu-sáa | ມະຄະບູຊາ |

This day is celebrated on the full moon of the third lunar month to commemorate the preaching of the Buddha to 1250 enlightened monks who came to hear him 'without prior summons'. A public holiday throughout the country, it culminates in a candle-lit walk around the main chapel at every wat.

## late january to early march

| | | |
|---|---|---|
| **Chinese New Year; Vietnamese Tet** | kút jíin | ກຸດຈີນ |

Chinese and Vietnamese populations all over Laos celebrate their lunar new year (the date shifts from year to year) with a

BASICS

week of house-cleaning, lion dances and fireworks. The most impressive festivities take place in Vientiane, Pakse and Savannakhet, with parties, deafening nonstop fireworks and visits to Vietnamese and Chinese temples. Chinese- and Vietnamese-run businesses usually close for three days.

## april

**Lao New Year** pịi mai láo ປີໃໝ່ລາວ

The lunar new year begins in mid-April and practically the entire country comes to a halt and celebrates. Houses are cleaned, people put on new clothes and Buddha images are washed with lustral water. In the wats, offerings of fruit and flowers are made at various altars and votive mounds of sand or stone are fashioned in the courtyards. Later the citizens take to the streets and dowse one another with water, which is an appropriate activity as April is usually the hottest month of the year. This festival is particularly picturesque in Luang Prabang, where it includes elephant processions. The 15th, 16th and 17th of April are official public holidays.

## may (full moon)

**Visakha Puja** wi-săa-khá bụu-sáa ວິສາຂະບູຊາ

This public holiday falls on the 15th day of the waxing moon in the sixth lunar month. It is considered the date of the Buddha's birth, enlightenment and parinibbana, or passing away. Activities are centred around the wat, with candle-lit processions, much chanting and sermonising.

**Rocket Festival** bụn bâng fái ບຸນບັ້ງໄຟ

This is a pre-Buddhist rain ceremony that is now celebrated alongside Visakha Puja in Laos and north-east Thailand. This can be one of the wildest festivals in the country, with plenty of music and dance (especially the irreverent mǎw lám (ໝໍລຳ) performances) processions and general merrymaking, culminating in the firing of bamboo rockets into the sky. In some places, male participants blacken their bodies with lamp soot, while women wear sunglasses and carry carved wooden phalli to imitate men. The firing of the rockets is supposed to prompt the heavens to initiate the rainy season and bring much-needed water to the rice fields.

## july

**Asanha Puja** ạa-sǎn-há bụu-sáa ອາສັນຫະບູຊາ

This public holiday commemorates the first sermon preached by the Buddha.

## mid to late july (full moon)

**Rains Retreat Opening** khào phán-sǎa (khào wat-sǎa) ເຂົ້າພັນສາ (ເຂົ້າວັດສາ)

This is the beginning of the traditional three-month 'rains retreat', during which Buddhist monks are expected to station themselves in a single monastery. At other times of year they are allowed to travel from wat to wat or simply to wander in the countryside, but during the rainy season they forego the wandering so as not to damage fields of rice or other crops. This is also the traditional time of year for men to enter the monkhood temporarily, hence many ordinations take place.

## august/september (full moon)

**Ancestor Respect** haw khào pá-dáp dịn ຫໍ່ເຂົ້າປະດັບດິນ

This is a sombre festival in which the living pay respect to the dead. Many cremations take place during this time and gifts are presented to the Sangha (Buddhist clergy) so that monks will chant on behalf of the deceased. Families visit bone stupas (ທາດກະດູກ, thàat ká-dùuk) with offerings of candles, incense and flowers.

## october/november (full moon)

| | | |
|---|---|---|
| **Rains Retreat Closing** | àwk phán-săa (àwk wat-săa) | ອອກພັນສາ (ອອກວັດສາ) |

This celebrates the end of the 3-month Rains Retreat. Monks are allowed to leave the monasteries to travel and are presented with robes, alms-bowls and other requisites of the renunciative life. A second festival held in association with Awk Phansaa is the Bụn Nâam (Water Festival). Boat races are commonly held in towns located on rivers, such as Vientiane, Luang Prabang and Savannakhet.

| | | |
|---|---|---|
| **Pha That Luang Festival** | bụn pha thâat lŭang | ບຸນພະທາດຫລວງ |

This takes place at Pha That Luang in Vientiane. Hundreds of monks assemble to receive alms and floral votives early in the morning on the first day of the festival, and there's a colourful procession between Pha That Luang and Wat Si Muang. The celebration lasts a week and includes fireworks and music, culminating in a candlelit circumambulation of That Luang.

## december

| | | |
|---|---|---|
| **Lao National Day** | wán sâat láo | ວັນຊາດລາວ |

The 2nd of December marks the 1975 victory of the proletariat over the monarchy with parades and speeches. It is a public holiday.

## december/january

| | | |
|---|---|---|
| **Prince Vessantara Festival** | bụn pha wêht | ບຸນພະເວດ |

This is a temple-centred festival in which the jataka or birth-tale of Prince Vessantara, the Buddha's penultimate life, is recited. This is also a favoured time (second to khào phán-săa) for Lao males to be ordained into the monkhood. The scheduling of Bun Pha Wet is staggered so that it is held on different days in different villages. This is so that relatives and friends living in different villages can invite one another to their respective celebrations.

| | | |
|---|---|---|
| **New Year's Day** | wán pịi mai sǎa-kọn | ວັນປີໃໝ່ສາກົນ |

A recent public holiday in deference to the Western calendar.

## useful words & phrases

ບາງຄຳສັບແລະປະໂຫຍກທີ່ເປັນປະໂຫຍດ

| | | |
|---|---|---|
| always | lêuay lêuay | ເລື້ອຍໆ |
| annual | thuk pịi | ທຸກປີ |
| before | kawn | ກ່ອນ |
| century | sá-tá-wat | ສະຕະວັດ |
| closed | pít | ປິດ |
| dawn | tạa-wán khèun | ຕາວັນຂຶ້ນ |
| daytime | kạang wán | ກາງວັນ |
| early | sâo | ເຊົ້າ |
| evening | láeng | ແລງ |
| every day | thuk wán | ທຸກວັນ |
| forever | tá-làwt kạan | ຕະຫລອດການ |
| holiday | wán phak kạan | ວັນພັກການ |
| late | sâa | ຊ້າ |
| night | khám | ຄ່ຳ |
| now | diaw nîi; tạwn nîi | ດຽວນີ້/ຕອນນີ້ |
| nowadays | sá-mǎi nîi | ສະໄໝນີ້ |
| open | pòet | ເປີດ |
| period (era) | sá-mǎi | ສະໄໝ |
| period (interval) | wéh-láa | ເວລາ |
| sometimes | bạang theua | ບາງເທື່ອ |
| time | wéh-láa | ເວລາ |
| on time | kọng taw wéh-láa | ກົງຕໍ່ເວລາ |
| in time | seu wéh-láa | ຊື່ເວລາ |
| until | jọn kwaa | ຈົນກ່ວາ |
| when (conjunction) | mêua/wéh-láa | ເມື່ອ/ເວລາ |
| when (what date?) | mêua-dại | ເມື່ອໃດ |
| whenever | mêua-dại kaw-tạam | ເມື່ອໃດກໍ່ຕາມ |

BASICS

## finding your way

ການຊອກທິດທາງ

Street signs in cities and towns in Laos are mostly written in Lao script only, although signs at major intersections in Vientiane are also written in French. The French designations for street names vary (eg, route, rue and avenue), but the Lao script always reads tha-nǒn (ຖະໜົນ), which means the same as all the French and English variations. Therefore, when asking directions it's always best to avoid possible confusion and use the Lao word tha-nǒn.

**Excuse me, can you help me?**
khǎw thôht, suay khàwy dâi baw — ຂໍໂທດ ຊ່ວຍຂ້ອຍໄດ້ບໍ່

| | | |
|---|---|---|
| **Where's the ...?** | ... yùu sǎi | ... ຢູ່ໃສ |
| **bus station** | sá-thǎa-níi lot pá-jąm tháang | ສະຖານີລົດປະຈຳທາງ |
| **bus stop** | bawn jàwt lot pá-jąm tháang | ບ່ອນຈອດລົດປະຈຳທາງ |
| **taxi stand** | bawn jàwt lot thaek-sîi | ບ່ອນຈອດລົດແທັກຊີ |
| **Which ... is this?** | bawn nîi maen ... nyǎng | ບ່ອນນີ້ແມ່ນ ... ຫຍັງ |
| **street/road** | tha-nǒn | ຖະໜົນ |
| **city** | méuang | ເມືອງ |
| **province** | khwǎeng | ແຂວງ |
| **village** | muu bâan | ໝູ່ບ້ານ |
| **I want to go to ...** | khàwy yàak pąi ... | ຂ້ອຍຢາກໄປ ... |
| **I'm looking for ...** | khàwy sâwk hǎa ... | ຂ້ອຍຊອກຫາ ... |
| **What time will the ... leave?** | ... já àwk ják móhng | ... ຈະອອກຈັກໂມງ |

| | | |
|---|---|---|
| aeroplane | héua bịn | ເຮືອບິນ |
| boat | héua | ເຮືອ |
| minivan | lot tûu | ລົດຕູ້ |

## directions

ທິດທາງ

| | | |
|---|---|---|
| **Excuse me, I'm looking for ...** | | |
| khǎw thôht, khàwy sâwk hǎa ... | | ຂໍໂທດ ຂ້ອຍຊອກຫາ ... |
| **How many kilometres from here?** | | |
| jàak nîi pại ják kí-lóh-maet | | ຈາກນີ້ໄປຈັກກິໂລແມັດ |
| Turn ... | lîaw ... | ລ້ຽວ ... |
| left | sâai | ຊ້າຍ |
| right | khwǎa | ຂວາ |
| Go straight ahead. | pại seu-seu | ໄປຊື່ໆ |
| Turn around. | lîaw káp | ລ້ຽວກັບ |
| Turn back. | káp máa | ກັບມາ |
| How far? | kại thao dại | ໄກເທົ່າໃດ |
| (not) far | (baw) kại | (ບໍ່) ໄກ |
| (not) near | (baw) kâi | (ບໍ່) ບໍ່ໄກ້ |
| north | thit něua | ທິດເໜືອ |
| south | thit tâi | ທິດໃຕ້ |
| east | thit tạa-wén àwk | ທິດຕາເວັນອອກ |
| west | thit tạa-wén tók | ທິດຕາເວັນຕົກ |

PRACTICAL

### street talk

Street addresses are rarely used in Laos outside of Vientiane. Even in the capital city, jumbo drivers may be unable to locate a specific street address, since the numbering of buildings – both residential and commercial – tends to follow the order of construction, not the position of a building on a street.

Tha-nŏn (ຖະໜົນ) is the general all-purpose Lao word meaning street, road, avenue and so on. A typical street address – where they exist – might be 69 Thanon Lan Xang.

Outside of the central Chanthabuli méuang (ເມືອງ, roughly, 'district') of Vientiane, few streets in Laos have signs bearing the name of the street. When such signs do exist, they are usually in Lao script only.

The méuang of Vientiane are broken up into bâan (ບ້ານ), which are neighbourhoods or villages associated with local wats. Wattay International Airport, for example, is in Ban Wat Tai, a village in the southern part of Muang Sikhottabong centred around Wat Tai.

## buying tickets

ການຊື້ແລະການຈອງປີ້

**I would like a ticket.**
khàwy yàak dâi pîi — ຂ້ອຍຢາກໄດ້ປີ້

**I would like two tickets.**
khàwy yàak dâi pîi sǎwng bại — ຂ້ອຍຢາກໄດ້ປີ້ສອງໃບ

**Are there any tickets to ...?**
mii pîi pại ... — ມີປີ້ໄປ ...

**How much per place (seat, deck space, etc)?**
bawn-la thao dại — ບ່ອນລະເທົ່າໃດ

**How many departures ... are there ...?** míi ják thîaw — ... ມີຈັກຖ້ຽວ

| | | |
|---|---|---|
| today | mêu nîi |  |
| tomorrow | mêu eun | ມື້ອື່ນ |

getting around

We would like to reserve ... places.
phûak háo yàak jąwng bawn ... bawn — ພວກເຮົາຢາກຈອງບ່ອນ ... ບ່ອນ

I'd like to change my ticket.
khàwy yàak pian pîi — ຂ້ອຍຢາກປ່ຽນປີ້

I'd like a refund on my ticket.
khàwy yàak khéun pîi — ຂ້ອຍຢາກຄືນປີ້

I'm sorry, I've changed my mind.
khǎw thôht, khàwy pian jąi lâew — ຂໍໂທດຂ້ອຍປ່ຽນໃຈແລ້ວ

## air

ທາງອາກາດ

Lao Aviation handles all domestic flights in Laos. You can purchase domestic tickets and make reservations at airline offices or travel agencies in every city that has an airfield.

| | | |
|---|---|---|
| aeroplane | héua bįn; nyón | ເຮືອບິນ; ຍົນ |
| airlines | kąan-bįn | ການບິນ |
| airport | doen bįn | ເດີນບິນ |
| departures/flights | thîaw bįn | ຖ້ຽວບິນ |
| Lao Aviation | kąan-bįn láo | ການບິນລາວ |
| plane tickets | pîi héua bįn; pîi nyón | ປີ້ເຮືອບິນ; ປີ້ຍົນ |

Is there a flight to ...?
míi thîaw bįn pąi ... — ມີຖ້ຽວບິນໄປ ...

When's the next flight to ...?
wéh-láa dąi míi thîaw bįn taw pąi ... — ເວລາໃດມີຖ້ຽວບິນຕໍ່ໄປ ...

What time will the plane leave?
héua bįn si khèun ják móhng — ເຮືອບິນຊິຂຶ້ນຈັກໂມງ

How long does the flight take?
sâi wéh-láa bįn dọn pąan dąi — ໃຊ້ເວລາບິນດົນປານໃດ

## bus

ລົດເມ

Where roads are surfaced, buses are an inexpensive and very acceptable way to get from one point to another. Outside the Mekong River Valley, Soviet, Vietnamese or Japanese trucks are often converted into passenger carriers by adding two long benches in the back. These passenger trucks are called tháek-síi (ແທັກຊີ, taxis), or in some areas sǎwng-thǎew (ສອງແຖວ, songthaew), which means 'two rows', in reference to the benches in the back.

Where public bus service isn't available, the Lao often travel long road distances by arranging rides with trucks carrying cargo from one province to another.

**bus station**
sá-thǎa-níi lot pá-jạm tháang (khíu lot méh) — ສະຖານີລົດປະຈຳທາງ (ຄິວລົດເມ)

**Which bus goes to ...?**
lot khán dại pai ... — ລົດຄັນໃດໄປ ...

**Does this bus go to ...?**
lot khán nîi pai ... baw — ລົດຄັນນີ້ໄປ ... ບໍ່

**How many departures are there today/tomorrow?**
mêu-nîi/mêu-eun míi ják thîaw — ມື້ນີ້/ມື້ອື່ນ ມີຈັກຖ້ຽວ

**What time will the bus leave?**
lot já àwk ják móhng — ລົດຈະອອກຈັກໂມງ

| | | |
|---|---|---|
| **What time's the ... bus?** | lot ... àwk ják móhng | ລົດ ... ອອກຈັກໂມງ |
| **first** | khán thii neung | ຄັນທີໜຶ່ງ |
| **last** | khán sut-thâai | ຄັນສຸດທ້າຍ |
| **next** | khán taw pại | ຄັນຕໍ່ໄປ |

**Could you tell me when we get to ...?**
jâo suay bàwk khàwy dâi baw wéh-láa pai hâwt ... — ເຈົ້າຊ່ວຍບອກຂ້ອຍໄດ້ບໍ່ ເວລາໄປຮອດ ...

**I want to get off.**
khàwy yàak lóng — ຂ້ອຍຢາກລົງ

## taxi

ລົດແທັກຊີ

Each of the country's three largest towns – Vientiane, Luang Prabang and Savannakhet – has a handful of car taxis that are used by foreign businesspeople and the occasional tourist. The only place you'll find these taxis is at the airports (arrival times only) and in front of the larger hotels. Taxis like these can be hired by the trip, by the hour or by the day.

| taxi | lot thâek-síi | ລົດແທັກຊີ |
|---|---|---|

## samlors & jumbos

ສາມລໍ້ແລະຈໍາໂບ້

Once a mainstay of local transport throughout urban Laos, the bicycle samlor has all but disappeared. When you can find them, samlor fares cost about the same as motorcycle taxis but are generally used only for distances less than 2km or so.

Three-wheeled motorcycle taxis are common in large cities. This type of vehicle can be called thâek-síi (ແທັກຊີ, taxi) or săam-lâw (ສາມລໍ້, 'three-wheels'). The larger ones made in Thailand are called jąm-bǫh (ຈໍາໂບ້, 'jumbos') and can hold four to six passengers. In Vientiane they are also sometimes called túk-túk (ຕຸກໆ) as in Thailand, while in the south (Pakse, Savannakhet) they may be called 'Skylab' because of the perceived resemblance to a space capsule! They can go anywhere a regular taxi can go, but aren't usually hired for distances greater than 20km or so.

PRACTICAL

## out for a ten count

| | | |
|---|---|---|
| 1 | neung | ໜຶ່ງ |
| 2 | sǎwng | ສອງ |
| 3 | sǎam | ສາມ |
| 4 | sii | ສີ່ |
| 5 | hàa | ຫ້າ |
| 6 | hók | ຫົກ |
| 7 | jét | ເຈັດ |
| 8 | pàet | ແປດ |
| 9 | kâo | ເກົ້າ |
| 10 | síp | ສິບ |

| | | |
|---|---|---|
| jumbo | jạm-bọh | ຈຳໂບ້ |
| samlor (pedicab) | sǎam-lâw | ສາມລໍ້ |

**How much to ...?**
pại ... thao dại — ໄປ ... ເທົ່າໃດ

**Too expensive. How about ... kìp?**
pháeng phôht. ... kíp dâi baw — ແພງໂພດ ... ກີບໄດ້ບໍ່

**Agreed. Let's go.**
tók-lóng. lâew pại — ຕົກລົງ ແລ້ວໄປ

**Drive slowly please.**
ká-lu-náa kháp sâa-sâa dae — ກະລຸນາຂັບຊ້າໆແດ່

**Continue!**
kháp taw pại iik — ຂັບຕໍ່ໄປອີກ

**Take the next street to the left/right.**
hâwt tháang taw pại lâew lîaw sâai/khwǎa — ຮອດທາງຕໍ່ໄປແລ້ວ ລ້ຽວຊ້າຍ/ຂວາ

**Please wait here.**
ká-lu-náa thàa yuu nîi — ກະລຸນາຖ້າຢູ່ນີ້

**Stop at the corner.**
ká-lu-náa jàwt yuu múum nîi — ກະລຸນາຈອດຢູ່ມູມນີ້

**Stop here.**
jàwt yuu nîi — ຈອດຢູ່ນີ້

# boat

ເຮືອ

Rivers are the traditional highways and byways of Laos, the main thoroughfares being the Mekong, Nam Ou, Nam Khan, Nam Tha, Nam Ngum and Se Don. The Mekong is the longest and most important water route and is navigable year-round between Luang Prabang in the north and Don Khong in the south.

For long distances, large diesel river ferries with overnight accommodation are used. For shorter river trips (eg, from Luang Prabang to the Pak Ou caves), it's usually best to hire a river taxi, since the large river ferries only ply their routes a couple of times a week. The longtail boats, with engines gimbal-mounted on the stern, are the most typical, though for a really short trip, such as crossing a river, a rowboat can be hired.

Along the upper Mekong River between Luang Prabang and Huay Sai, Thai-built speedboats – shallow, five-metre-long skiffs with 40-hp outboard engines – are common.

| | | |
|---|---|---|
| **boat** | héua | ເຮືອ |
| **boat taxi** | héua jâang | ເຮືອຈ້າງ |
| **cross-river ferry** | héua khàam fâak;<br>héua bák | ເຮືອຂ້າມຟາກ/<br>ເຮືອບັກ |
| **longtail boat** | héua hăang nyáo | ເຮືອຫາງຍາວ |
| **row boat** | héua phái | ເຮືອພາຍ |
| **speed boat** | héua wái | ເຮືອໄວ |

**Where do we get on the boat?**
lóng héua yuu săi — ລົງເຮືອຢູ່ໃສ

**What time does the boat leave?**
héua já àwk ják móhng — ເຮືອຈະອອກຈັກໂມງ

**What time does the boat arrive?**
héua já máa hâwt ják móhng — ເຮືອຈະມາຮອດຈັກໂມງ

## useful words & phrases

ຄຳສັບແລະປະໂຫຍກທີ່ເປັນປະໂຫຍດ

| | | |
|---|---|---|
| **arrive** | máa hâwt | ມາຮອດ |
| **bridge** | khŭa | ຂົວ |
| **charter vehicle** | lot jâang | ລົດຈ້າງ |
| **daily** | pá-jąm mêu (thuk mêu) | ປະຈຳມື້ (ທຸກມື້) |
| **detour** | tháang wêhn | ທາງເວັ້ນ |
| **drive** | kháp | ຂັບ |
| **early** | sâo | ເຊົ້າ |
| **fast** | wái | ໄວ |
| **hire/charter** | jâang | ຈ້າງ |
| **leave** | àwk | ອອກ |
| **pier** | thaa héua | ທ່າເຮືອ |
| **'regular vehicle' (ie, not a charter vehicle)** | lot pá-jąm | ລົດປະຈຳ |
| **seat** | bawn nang | ບ່ອນນັ່ງ |
| **slow** | sâa | ຊ້າ |
| **stop/park** | jàwt | ຈອດ |

**What time does it leave here?**
já àwk jàak nîi ják móhng — ຈະອອກຈາກນີ້ຈັກໂມງ

**What time does it arrive there?**
já pąi hâwt phûn ják móhng — ຈະໄປຮອດພຸ້ນຈັກໂມງ

**What time does the first vehicle leave?**
khán thii neung já àwk ják móhng — ຄັນທີ່ໜຶ່ງຈະອອກຈັກໂມງ

**What time does the last vehicle leave?**
khán sút-thâai já àwk ják móhng — ຄັນສຸດທ້າຍຈະອອກຈັກໂມງ

What's the fare?
khaa dọen tháang thao dại — ຄ່າເດີນທາງເທົ່າໃດ

How much per person?
khón-la thao dại — ຄົນລະເທົ່າໃດ

I/We don't want to charter a vehicle.
baw yàak jâang lot — ບໍ່ຢາກຈ້າງລົດ

I/We want to charter a vehicle.
yàak jâang lot — ຢາກຈ້າງລົດ

Can you lower the price?
lut láa-kháa dâi baw — ລຸດລາຄາໄດ້ບໍ່

Can you lower (the price) more?
lut ìik dâi baw — ລຸດອີກໄດ້ບໍ່

Where does the vehicle depart from?
lot àwk yuu săi — ລົດອອກຢູ່ໃສ

Where can we get on the vehicle?
khèun lot yuu săi — ຂຶ້ນລົດຢູ່ໃສ

Is there anyone sitting here?
mii phăi nang yuu nîi baw — ມີໃຜນັ່ງຢູ່ນີ້ບໍ່

May I sit here?
nang bawn nîi dâi baw — ນັ່ງບ່ອນນີ້ໄດ້ບໍ່

Can I put my bag here?
wáang thŏng yuu nîi dâi baw — ວາງຖົງຢູ່ນີ້ໄດ້ບໍ່

Can you wait for me?
thàa khàwy dâi baw — ຖ້າຂ້ອຍໄດ້ບໍ່

Can you wait here?
jâo thàa yuu nîi dâi baw — ເຈົ້າຖ້າຢູ່ນີ້ໄດ້ບໍ່

Where are you going?
pại săi — ໄປໃສ

I want to go to ...
khàwy yàak pại ... — ຂ້ອຍຢາກໄປ ...

I'll get out here.
khàwy si long bawn nîi — ຂ້ອຍຊິລົງບ່ອນນີ້

PRACTICAL

## waving the flag

Laos' national seal, often applied to official government publications, features a near-complete circle formed by curving rice stalks which enclose six component symbols of the productive proletarian state: Vientiane's Pha That Luang (representing religion); a checkerboard of rice fields (agriculture); gear cogs (industry); a dam (energy); a highway (transport); and a grove of trees (forestry). A label in Lao script at the bottom of the seal reads 'Lao People's Democratic Republic'.

The national flag consists of two horizontal bars of red (symbolising courage and heroism), above and below a bar of blue (nationhood) on which is centred a blank white sphere (the light of communism), sometimes also interpreted as a moon. This flag is flown in front of all government offices and by some private citizens on National Day (2 December). On this holiday the Lao national flag may be joined by a second flag featuring a yellow hammer and sickle centred on a field of red, the international symbol of communism.

**Which vehicle goes to ...?**
lot khan dại pại ... — ລົດຄັນໃດໄປ ...

**When we arrive in ..., please tell me.**
wéh-láa hâwt ... bàwk khàwy dae — ເວລາຮອດ ... ບອກຂ້ອຍແດ່

**Can we stop over in ...?**
long phak yuu ... dâi baw — ລົງພັກຢູ່ ... ໄດ້ບໍ່

**Stop here.**
jàwt bawn nîi — ຈອດບ່ອນນີ້

## renting vehicles

ການເຊົ່າລົດ, ລົດຈັກແລະລົດຖີບ

Cars, motorcycles and bicycles can be rented in Vientiane and to a lesser degree in Luang Prabang. Bicycles can usually be arranged in smaller towns and are a good way of getting around since traffic is relatively light.

| | | |
|---|---|---|
| I'd like to rent a ... | khàwy yàak sao ... | ຂ້ອຍຢາກເຊົ່າ ... |
| bicycle | lot thìip | ລົດຖີບ |
| car | lot ọh-tọh | ລົດໂອໂຕ |
| motorcycle | lot ják | ລົດຈັກ |
| truck | lot bạn-thuk | ລົດບັນທຸກ |
| How much per/for ...? | thao dại | ... ເທົ່າໃດ |
| hour | sua-móhng-la | ຊົ່ວໂມງລະ |
| day | mêu-la | ມື້ລະ |
| week | ạa-thit-la | ອາທິດລະ |
| month | dẹuan-la | ເດືອນລະ |
| three days | săam mêu | ສາມມື້ |

**Does the price include insurance?**
láa-kháa huam nám pá-kạn phái baw
ລາຄາຮ່ວມນຳປະກັນໄພບໍ່

**Where's the next petrol station?**
pâm nâm-mán taw pại yuu sǎi
ປ້ຳນ້ຳມັນຕໍ່ໄປຢູ່ໃສ

**Please fill the tank.**
ká-lu-náa sai nâm-man hài tem thăng
ກະລຸນາໃສ່ ນ້ຳມັນໃຫ້ເຕັມຖັງ

**I'd like ... litres.**
sai ... lit
ໃສ່ ... ລິດ

**Does this road lead to ...?**
tháang nîi pại hâwt ... baw
ທາງນີ້ໄປຮອດ ... ບໍ່

| | | |
|---|---|---|
| Please check the ... | ká-lu-náa kùat ... | ກະລຸນາກວດ ... |
| air | lóm | ລົມ |
| oil | nâm-mán | ນ້ຳມັນ |
| water | nâm | ນ້ຳ |
| tyre pressure | khwáam dạn khǎwng yáang lot | ຄວາມດັນ ຂອງຢາງລົດ |

## car problems

ບັນຫາລົດ

We need a mechanic.
phûak háo tâwng-kạan saang pạeng ják — ພວກເຮົາຕ້ອງການ ຊ່າງແປງຈັກ

What make is it?
yii hàw nyǎng — ຍີ່ຫໍ້ຫຍັງ

Can you repair it?
jâo pạeng dâi baw — ເຈົ້າແປງໄດ້ບໍ່

The battery's flat.
màw fái awn — ໝໍ້ໄຟອ່ອນ

I have a flat tyre.
yáang lot khàwy hua — ຢາງລົດຂ້ອຍຮົ່ວ

It's overheating.
mán hâwn lǎai phôht — ມັນຮ້ອນຫລາຍໂພດ

The radiator's leaking.
màw nâm hua — ໝໍ້ນ້ຳຮົ່ວ

It's not working.
mán baw het wîak — ມັນບໍ່ເຮັດວຽກ

getting around

## useful words

ສັບທີ່ເປັນປະໂຫຍດ

| | | |
|---|---|---|
| battery | màw fái | ໝໍ້ໄຟ |
| brakes | hàam | ຫ້າມ |
| clutch | khâat | ຄາດ |
| drivers licence | bại á-nu-nyâat kháp khii | ໃບອະນຸຍາດຂັບຂີ່ |
| engine | kheuang ják | ເຄືອງຈັກ |
| garage | uu sàwm pạeng lot | ອູ່ສ້ອມແປງລົດ |
| headlight | fái tạa tháang nàa | ໄຟຕາທາງໜ້າ |
| insurance | pá-kạn phái | ປະກັນໄພ |
| lights | fái | ໄຟ |
| mechanic | saang pạeng ják | ຊ່າງແປງຈັກ |
| motor oil | nâm-mán kheuang | ນ້ຳມັນເຄືອງ |
| oil | nâm-mán | ນ້ຳມັນ |
| petrol (gasoline) | nâm-mán (áet-sáng) | ນ້ຳມັນ (ແອັດຊັງ) |
| petrol station | pâm nâm-mán | ປ້ຳນ້ຳມັນ |
| puncture | hua/jáw | ຮົ່ວ/ເຈາະ |
| radiator | màw nâm | ໝໍ້ນ້ຳ |
| tyre | yạang lot | ຢາງລົດ |
| wheel | lâw | ລໍ້ |
| windscreen | waen nàa | ແຫວ່ນໜ້າ |

# accommodation

ສະຖານທີ່ພັກແຮມ

In Laos, generally speaking, a 'single' means a room with one large bed that will sleep two, while a 'double' has two large beds. Room rates are thus quoted according to the number of beds a room has, rather than the number of guests who will be using the room. This is especially true for guesthouses. On the other hand, a few larger, Western-style hotels do calculate room tariffs according to the number of guests per room.

An 'ordinary room' (ຫ້ອງທຳມະດາ, hàwng thám-ma-dąa) usually means a less expensive room with a fan rather than with air-conditioning.

If you find yourself in a town or village where no hotels or guesthouses are available, or where they are all full, you may be invited to stay with local residents. In such cases you may be asked for a small fee. If not, it's good form to offer a gift – preferably food or something needed in the household – to your hosts.

## finding accommodation

ການຊອກສະຖານທີ່ພັກແຮມ

| | | |
|---|---|---|
| **hotel** | hóhng háem | ໂຮງແຮມ |
| **guesthouse** | héuan phak | ເຮືອນພັກ |

**Excuse me, is there a hotel nearby?**
khǎw thôht, mįi hóhng háem yuu kâi nîi baw
ຂໍໂທດ ມີໂຮງແຮມ ຢູ່ໃກ້ນີ້ບໍ່

**Is this a hotel?**
nîi maen hóhng háem baw
ນີ້ແມ່ນໂຮງແຮມບໍ່

**Is this a guesthouse?**
nîi maen héuan phak baw
ນີ້ແມ່ນເຮືອນພັກບໍ່

**Is there a place to stay here?**
yuu nîi míi bawn phak baw
ຢູ່ນີ້ມີບ່ອນພັກບໍ່

We need a place to stay.
phûak háo tâwng-kạan bawn phak — ພວກເຮົາຕ້ອງການບ່ອນພັກ

Can I/we stay here?
phak yuu nîi dâi baw — ພັກຢູ່ນີ້ໄດ້ບໍ່

Can I/we sleep here?
náwn yuu nîi dâi baw — ນອນຢູ່ນີ້ໄດ້ບໍ່

## checking in

ການແຈ້ງເຂົ້າ

| | | |
|---|---|---|
| air-conditioning | ạe yẹn | ແອເຢັນ |
| bathroom | hàwng nâm | ຫ້ອງນ້ຳ |
| double room | hàwng náwn tịang khuu | ຫ້ອງນອນຕຽງຄູ່ |
| fan | phat lóm | ພັດລົມ |
| hot water | nâm hâwn | ນ້ຳຮ້ອນ |
| not vacant | baw waang | ບໍ່ຫວ້າງ |
| room | hàwng | ຫ້ອງ |
| single room | hàwng náwn tịang diaw | ຫ້ອງນອນຕຽງດ່ຽວ |
| toilet | sùam | ສ້ວມ |
| vacant | waang | ຫວ້າງ |

Do you have a room?
míi hàwng baw — ມີຫ້ອງບໍ່

How many people?
ják khón — ຈັກຄົນ

one person
neung khón; khón diaw — ໜຶ່ງຄົນ; ຄົນດຽວ

two people
sǎwng khón — ສອງຄົນ

| | | |
|---|---|---|
| How much per/for ...? | ... thao dại | ... ເທົ່າໃດ |
| night | khéun-la | ຄືນລະ |
| week | ạa-thit-la | ອາທິດລະ |
| month | dèuan-la | ເດືອນລະ |
| three nights | sǎam khéun | ສາມຄືນ |

PRACTICAL

## wit & wisdom

**It's easy to earn money but difficult to find kindness.**

ngóen khám hǎa dâi, nâm jại hǎa nຫyàak — ເງິນຄຳຫາໄດ້ ນ້ຳໃຈຫາຍາກ

**It's too expensive.**
pháeng phôht — ແພງໂພດ

**I/We will stay two nights.**
síi phak sǎwng khéun — ຊິພັກສອງຄືນ

**Can you lower the price?**
lut láa-kháa dâi baw — ລຸດລາຄາໄດ້ບໍ່

**Can I/we look at the room?**
khaw boeng hàwng dâi baw — ຂໍເບິ່ງຫ້ອງໄດ້ບໍ່

**Do you have any other rooms?**
míi hàwng eun íik baw — ມີຫ້ອງອື່ນອີກບໍ່

**I/We want an ordinary room.**
ạo hàwng thám-ma-dạa — ເອົາຫ້ອງທຳມະດາ

| | | |
|---|---|---|
| **We need a ... room than this.** | phûak háo tâwng-kạan hàwng ... nîi | ພວກເຮົາ ຕ້ອງການຫ້ອງ ... ນີ້ |
| **cheaper** | théuk-kwaa | ຖືກກວ່າ |
| **larger** | nyai-kwaa | ໃຫຍ່ກວ່າ |
| **smaller** | nâwy-kwaa | ນ້ອຍກວ່າ |
| **quieter** | mit-kwaa | ມິດກວ່າ |

## requests & complaints

ການຮ້ອງຂໍ ແລະຕໍ່ວ່າ

| | | |
|---|---|---|
| Is there ...? | mîi ... baw | ມີ ... ບໍ່ |
| a telephone | thóh-la-sáp | ໂທລະສັບ |
| hot water | nâm hâwn | ນ້ຳຮ້ອນ |
| I/We need (a) ... | tâwng-kaan ... | ຕ້ອງການ ... |
| another bed | tiang ìik | ຕຽງອີກ |
| blanket | phàa hom | ຜ້າຫົ່ມ |
| key | ká-jae | ກະແຈ |
| pillow | măwn | ໝອນ |
| sheet | phàa puu bawn | ຜ້າປູບ່ອນ |
| soap | sá-buu | ສະບູ |
| towel | phàa set toh | ຜ້າເຊັດໂຕ |

Can you clean the room?
á-náa-mái hàwng hài dae dâi baw — ອະນາໄມຫ້ອງໃຫ້ແດ່ໄດ້ບໍ່

This room isn't clean.
hàwng nîi baw sá-àat — ຫ້ອງນີ້ບໍ່ສະອາດ

There's no hot water.
baw mîi nâm hâwn — ບໍ່ມີນ້ຳຮ້ອນ

Can you repair it?
jâo paeng hài dae dâi baw — ເຈົ້າແປງໃຫ້ແດ່ໄດ້ບໍ່

## checking out

ການແຈ້ງອອກ

| | | |
|---|---|---|
| bill | bai bin | ໃບບິນ |
| receipt | bai hap ngóen | ໃບຮັບເງິນ |
| service charge | khaa baw-li-kaan | ຄ່າບໍລິການ |
| tax | pháa-sĭi | ພາສີ |

I/We will return in two weeks.
ìik săwng aa-thit síi káp máa — ອີກສອງອາທິດຊິກັບມາ

Can I store my bags here?
fàak kheuang yuu nîi dâi baw — ຝາກເຄື່ອງຢູ່ນີ້ໄດ້ບໍ່

PRACTICAL

### yes, no, maybe...

'Yes' and 'No' don't exist in Lao in the same way as in English – it depends on the verb used in the question. Refer to page 39 for the basics on answering questions.

## laundry

ຊັກເຄື່ອງ

**Can you wash these clothes?**
sak séua phàa nîi dâi baw — ຊັກເສື້ອຜ້ານີ້ໄດ້ບໍ່

**Where can I wash my clothes (myself)?**
khàwy sak séua phàa ẹhng dâi yuu sǎi — ຂ້ອຍຊັກເສື້ອຜ້າ ເອງໄດ້ຢູ່ໃສ

**Is there a laundry near here?**
yuu thǎew nîi míi bawn sak lîit baw — ຢູ່ແຖວນີ້ມີບ່ອນ ຊັກລີດບໍ່

**No starch.**
baw lóng pâeng — ບໍ່ລົງແປ້ງ

**Add starch.**
lóng pâeng — ລົງແປ້ງ

**These clothes aren't very clean.**
séua phàa nîi baw sá-áat thao dại — ເສື້ອຜ້ານີ້ບໍ່ສະອາດເທົ່າໃດ

**Please wash them again.**
ká-lu-náa sak íik theua — ກະລຸນາຊັກອີກເທື່ອ

| | | |
|---|---|---|
| dry-clean | sak háeng | ຊັກແຫ້ງ |
| iron (n) | tạo lîit | ເຕົາລີດ |
| to iron | lîit | ລີດ |
| laundry service | bạw-li-kạan sak lîit | ບໍລິການຊັກລີດ |

## useful words

| | | ຄຳສັບທີ່ເປັນປະໂຫຍດ |
|---|---|---|
| accommodation | bawn phak | ບ່ອນພັກ |
| to bathe | áap nâm | ອາບນ້ຳ |
| bathroom | tịang náwn | ຕຽງນອນ |
| bedroom | hàwng náwn | ຫ້ອງນອນ |
| breakfast | ạa-hăan sâo | ອາຫານເຊົ້າ |
| electricity | fái fâa | ໄຟຟ້າ |
| elevator (lift) | lip | ລິບ |
| entrance | tháang khào | ທາງເຂົ້າ |
| exit | tháang àwk | ທາງອອກ |
| fan | phat lóm | ພັດລົມ |
| food | ạa-hăan | ອາຫານ |
| lights | fái | ໄຟ |

# around town

## ສະຖານທີ່ຕ່າງໆ ພາຍໃນເມືອງ

### looking for ...

ກຳລັງຊອກຫາ ...

| | | |
|---|---|---|
| Where is the ...? | ... yùu săi | ... ຢູ່ໃສ |
| How far is the ...? | ... kại thao dại | ... ໄກເທົ່າໃດ |
| I'm looking for the ... | khàwy sâwk hăa ... | ຂ້ອຍຊອກຫາ ... |
| art gallery | háan wáang sá-dạeng sĭ-la-pá | ຮ້ານວາງສະແດງສິລະປະ |
| barber shop | hâan tát phŏm | ຮ້ານຕັດຜົມ |
| Buddhist temple; monastery | wat | ວັດ |
| cemetery | paa sâa | ປ່າຊ້າ |
| church | bòht khlit | ໂບດຄລິດ |
| city centre | kạang méuang | ກາງເມືອງ |
| ... consulate | ... kọng-sŭun | ... ກົງສູນ |
| ... embassy | ... sa-thăan-thûut | ... ສະຖານທູດ |
| factory | hóhng ngáan | ໂຮງງານ |
| hotel | hóhng háem | ໂຮງແຮມ |
| market | ta-làat | ຕະຫລາດ |
| monument | á-nu-săa-wa-líi | ອານຸສາວະລີ |
| museum | phi-phit-tha-phán | ພິພິດທະພັນ |
| park (garden) | sŭan săa-tháa-la-na | ສວນສາທາລະນະ |
| police | tạm-lùat | ຕຳຫລວດ |
| post office | pại-sá-níi (hóhng săai) | ໄປສະນີ (ໂຮງສາຍ) |
| public telephone | thóh-la-sáp săa-tháa-la-na | ໂທລະສັບສາທາລະນະ |
| public toilet | hàwng nâm săa-tháa-la-na | ຫ້ອງນ້ຳສາທາລະນະ |
| school | hóhng hían | ໂຮງຮຽນ |
| telephone centre | sŭun thóh-la-sáp | ສູນໂທລະສັບ |
| tourist information office | hàwng khàw múun khao săan thawng thiaw | ຫ້ອງຂໍ້ມູນຂ່າວສານທ່ອງທ່ຽວ |

# at the bank

ຢູ່ທະນາຄານ

The official national currency in the LPDR is the kip (ກີບ, kìip). In reality, the people of Laos use three currencies in day-to-day commerce: kip, Thai baht and US dollars. Kip notes come in denominations of 100, 500, 1000, 2000 and 5000.

By and large, the best exchange rates are available at banks rather than moneychangers. Travellers cheques receive a slightly better exchange rate than cash. Banks in larger towns can change Euros, Canadian, US and Australian dollars, French francs, Thai baht and Japanese yen, while provincial banks will accept only US dollars or baht.

Many hotels, upscale restaurants and gift shops in Vientiane and Luang Prabang accept Visa or MasterCard. A few also accept American Express.

**I want to change money.**
khàwy yàak pian ngóen — ຂ້ອຍຢາກປ່ຽນເງິນ

**Can I/we change money here?**
pian ngóen yuu nîi dâi baw — ປ່ຽນເງິນຢູ່ນີ້ໄດ້ບໍ່

**What is the exchange rate?**
át-tạa lâek pian thao dại — ອັດຕາແລກປ່ຽນເທົ່າໃດ

**Can I get smaller change?**
khǎw pian ngóen nâwy dâi baw — ຂໍປ່ຽນເງິນນ້ອຍໄດ້ບໍ່

**I want to change ...**
khàwy yàak pian ... — ຂ້ອຍຢາກປ່ຽນ ...

| | | |
|---|---|---|
| **cash/money** | ngóen sót/ngóen | ເງິນສົດ/ເງິນ |
| **a cheque** | bại saek | ໃບແຊັກ |
| **a travellers cheque** | saek thawng thiaw | ແຊັກທ່ອງທ່ຽວ |

**Can I use my credit card to withdraw money?**
khàwy sâi bát khléh-dít thǎwn ngóen dâi baw — ຂ້ອຍໃຊ້ບັດຄູເຣດິດ ຖອນເງິນໄດ້ບໍ່

**What's your commission?**
jâo ào khâa bàw-li-kàan thao dại — ເຈົ້າເອົາຄ່າບໍລິການເທົ່າໃດ

**How many kip per dollar?**
ják kìip taw dọh-láa — ຈັກກີບ

**Can I get smaller change?**
khăw pian ngóen nâwy dâi baw — ຂໍປ່ຽນເງິນນ້ອຍໄດ້ບໍ່

**Can I transfer money here from my bank?**
khàwy ọhn ngóen jàak tha-náa-kháan khàwy máa nîi dâi baw — ຂ້ອຍໂອນເງິນຈາກທະນາຄານຂ້ອຍມານີ້ໄດ້ບໍ່

**How many days will it take to arrive?**
ják méu sii máa hâwt — ຈັກມື້ຊິມາຮອດ

**Has my money arrived yet?**
ngóen khàwy máa hâwt lâew baw — ເງິນຂ້ອຍມາຮອດແລ້ວບໍ່

**Can I transfer money overseas?**
khàwy ọhn ngóen pại taang pá-thêht dâi baw — ຂ້ອຍໂອນເງິນໄປຕ່າງປະເທດໄດ້ບໍ່

| | | |
|---|---|---|
| **I have ...** | khàwy míi ... | ຂ້ອຍມີ ... |
| **US$** | dọh-láa ạa-méh-li-kạa | ໂດລາອາເມລິກາ |
| **UK£** | pạwn ạng-kít | ປອນອັງກິດ |
| **A$** | dọh-láa ạw-sá-tạa-líi | ໂດລາອົດສຕາລີ |
| **HK$** | dọh-láa hong kọng | ໂດລາຮົງກົງ |
| **Euros** | yúu-lóh | ຢູໂລ |
| **¥en** | yéhn nyii-pun | ເຢັນຍີ່ປຸ່ນ |

| | | |
|---|---|---|
| **bank** | tha-náa-kháan | ທະນາຄານ |
| **change (n)** | ngóen nâwy | ເງິນນ້ອຍ |
| **to change** | lâek pian | ແລກປ່ຽນ |
| **check** | saek | ແຊັກ |
| **exchange rate** | át-tạa lâek pian | ອັດຕາແລກປ່ຽນ |
| **money** | ngóen | ເງິນ |

## at the post office

ຢູ່ຫ້ອງການໄປສະນ

Outgoing mail is fairly reliable and inexpensive. The safe arrival of incoming mail is less certain, especially for packages. When posting any package, even small padded mailers, you must leave the package open for inspection by a postal officer.

**Is this the post office?**
nîi maen pai-sá-níi baw — ນີ້ແມ່ນໄປສະນີບໍ່

**I want to send a ...**
khàwy yàak song ... — ຂ້ອຍຢາກສິ່ງ ...

| | | |
|---|---|---|
| letter | jót-măai | ຈິດໝາຍ |
| postcard | pai-sá-níi bát | ໄປສະນີບັດ |
| parcel | haw kheuang | ຫໍ່ເຄື່ອງ |
| telegram | thóh-la-lêhk | ໂທລະເລກ |

**Please send it by airmail/ surface mail.**
ká-lu-náa song tháang aa-kàat/thám-ma-dáa — ກະລຸນາສິ່ງທາງ ອາກາດ/ທຳມະດາ

**How much does it cost to send this to ...?**
láa-kháa thao-dai săm-láp song an-nîi pai ... — ລາຄາເທົ່າໃດສຳລັບ ສິ່ງອັນນີ້ໄປ...

**May I have (a/an/some) ...?**
khăw ... — ຂໍ ...

| | | |
|---|---|---|
| stamps | sa-taem | ສະແຕມ |
| envelope | sáwng jót-măai | ຊອງຈິດໝາຍ |
| insurance | pá-kan phái | ປະກັນໄພ |
| registered receipt | bai lóng tha-bian | ໃບລິງທະບຽນ |

PRACTICAL

**This letter is going to the (USA).**
jót-măai nîi pại (ạa-méh-li-kạa)
ຈົດໝາຍນີ້ໄປ ອາເມລິກາ

**How much to send this letter to (England)?**
song jót-măai nîi pại (ạng-kít) láa-kháa thao dại
ສົ່ງຈົດໝາຍນີ້ໄປອັງກິດ ລາຄາເທົ່າໃດ

**I'd like four 100 kip stamps, please.**
khăw sa-taem bại-la hàwy kìip sii ạn
ຂໍສະແຕມໃບລະ ຮ້ອຍກີບສີ່ອັນ

**I want to send this package by air mail.**
khàwy yàak song haw nîi pại tháang ạa-kàat
ຂ້ອຍຢາກສົ່ງຫໍ່ນີ້ໄປ ທາງອາກາດ

**I want a registered receipt.**
khàwy yàak dâi bại lóng tha-bịan
ຂ້ອຍຢາກໄດ້ໃບລົງ ທະບຽນ

**Where's the poste restante section?**
pawng bạw-li-kạan jót-măai sua kháo yuu săi
ປ່ອງບໍລິການຈົດໝາຍ ຊົ່ວຄາວຢູ່ໃສ

**Is there any mail for me?**
míi jót-măai khàwy baw
ມີຈົດໝາຍຂ້ອຍບໍ່

**My last name is ...**
náam sá-kụn khàwy máen ...
ນາມສະກຸນຂ້ອຍແມ່ນ ...

## useful words

ຄຳສັບທີ່ເປັນປະໂຫຍດ

| | | |
|---|---|---|
| **air (mail)** | tháang ạa-kàat | ທາງອາກາດ |
| **express (mail)** | tháang duan | ທາງດ່ວນ |
| **mail (n)** | jót-mǎai | ຈົດໝາຍ |
| **mail box** | tûu jót-mǎai | ຕູ້ຈົດໝາຍ |
| **postcode** | la-hat pại-sa-níi | ລະຫັດໄປສະນີ |
| **to register** | lóng tha-bịan | ìö¤ê½®¼$ |
| **registered mail** | jót-mǎai long tha-bịan | ຈົດໝາຍລົງ ທະບຽນ |
| **surface mail** | jót-mǎai tháang thám-ma-dạa | ຈົດໝາຍທາງ ທຳມະດາ |

## telephone

ໂທລະສັບ

The best place to make international calls is the International Telephone Office (Cabines Télécommuniques Internationales) on Thanon Setthathirat in Vientiane, which is open 24 hours a day. In provincial capitals, international telephone service is available at the GPO.

| | | |
|---|---|---|
| **international call** | thóh-la-sáp la-waang pá-thêht | ໂທລະສັບ ລະຫວ່າງປະເທດ |
| **long distance (domestic)** | tháang kại | ທາງໄກ |
| **minute(s)** | náa-thíi | ນາທີ |
| **mobile/cell phone** | thóh-la-sáp méu thěu | ໂທລະສັບມືຖື |
| **operator** | phùu taw sǎai | ຜູ້ຕໍ່ສາຍ |
| **phone book** | pêum thóh-la-sáp | ປຶ້ມໂທລະສັບ |
| **phone box** | káp thóh-la-sáp | ກັບໂທລະສັບ |
| **phonecard** | bát thóh-la-sáp | ບັດໂທລະສັບ |
| **telephone** | thóh-la-sáp | ໂທລະສັບ |
| **urgent** | duan | ດ່ວນ |

PRACTICAL

**How much does it cost to call Australia ...?**
thóh-la-sáp pại ạw-sá-tạa-líi láa-kháa thao dại
ໂທລະສັບໄປອົສຕາລີ ລາຄາເທົ່າໃດ

**I want to call ...**
khàwy yàak thóh ...
ຂ້ອຍຢາກໂທ ...

**I'd like to speak for 10 minutes.**
khàwy yàak thóh síp náa-thíi
ຂ້ອຍຢາກໂທສິບນາທີ

**How much does a (three)-minute call cost?**
khaa thóh (săam) náa-thíi thao dại
ຄ່າໂທ(ສາມ)ນາທີ ເທົ່າໃດ

**How much does each extra minute cost?**
kháa thóh phôem náa-thíi la thao dại
ຄ່າໂທເພີ້ມນາທີລະເທົ່າໃດ

**The number is ...**
bọe thóh maen ...
ເບີໂທແມ່ນ ...

**It's engaged.**
thóh-la-sáp baw waang
ໂທລະສັບບໍ່ຫ່ວາງ

**I've been cut off.**
thóh-la-sáp tàt
ໂທລະສັບຕັດ

## fax & telegraph

ໂທລະສານແລະໂທລະເລກ

Fax, telex and telegraph services are handled at the GPO in each provincial capital. Larger hotels with business centres offer the same telecommunication services but always at higher rates.

**How much per page?**
phaen-la thao dại
ແຜ່ນລະເທົ່າໃດ

**How much per word?**
khám-la thao dại
ຄຳລະເທົ່າໃດ

| | | |
|---|---|---|
| **fax** | fáek | ແຟັກ |
| **telegraph** | thóh-la-lêhk | ໂທລະເລກ |

## internet

ອິນເຕີແນັດ

**Is there a local Internet cafe?**
míi ịn-tọe-naet kạa-féh baw — ມີອິນເຕີແນັດກາເຟບໍ່

**I'd like to get Internet access.**
khàwy yàak sâi ịn-tọe-naet — ຂ້ອຍຢາກໃຊ້ອິນເຕີແນັດ

**I'd like to check my email.**
yàak kùat ịi-máew — ຢາກກວດອີແມວ

**I'd like to send an email.**
yàak song ịi-máew — ຢາກສົ່ງອີແມວ

| | | |
|---|---|---|
| computer | kháwm-pịi-tọe | ຄອມປິເຕີ |
| email | ịi-máew | ອີແມວ |
| modem | móh-dạem | ໂມແດມ |

## paperwork

ເອກະສານ

| | | |
|---|---|---|
| name | seu | ຊື່ |
| address | thii yuu | ທີ່ຢູ່ |
| date of birth | wán dẹuan pịi kòet | ວັນເດືອນປີເກີດ |
| place of birth | thii kòet | ທີ່ເກີດ |
| age | ạa-nyu | ອາຍຸ |
| sex | phêht | ເພດ |
| nationality | săn-sâat | ສັນຊາດ |
| religion | sàat-sá-náa | ສາສະນາ |
| profession/work | ạa-sîip | ອາຊີບ |
| reason for travel | jút-pa-sŏng dọen tháang | ຈຸດປະສົງເດີນທາງ |
| customs | dàan pháa-sĭi | ດ່ານພາສີ |

PRACTICAL

| | | |
|---|---|---|
| **marital status** | thǎa-na kạan taeng-ngáan | ຖານະ ການແຕ່ງງານ |
| **single** | sòht | ໂສດ |
| **married** | taeng-ngáan lâew | ແຕ່ງງານແລ້ວ |
| **divorced** | hâang lâew | ຮ້າງແລ້ວ |
| **widow** | mae màai | ແມ່ໝ້າຍ |
| **widower** | phaw màai | ພໍ່ໝ້າຍ |
| **identification** | bát pá-jạm tụa | ບັດປະຈຳຕົວ |
| **passport number** | nâm-bọe nǎng sěu phaan dạen | ນຳເບີ ໜັງສືຜ່ານແດນ |
| **visa** | wi-sáa | ວີຊາ |
| **drivers licence** | bại á-nu-nyâat kháp khii | ໃບອະນຸຍາດຂັບຂີ່ |
| **immigration** | kùat khón khào méuang | ກວດຄົນເຂົ້າເມືອງ |
| **purpose of visit** | jút pa-sǒng yîam yáam | ຈຸດປະສົງຢ້ຽມຢາມ |
| **business** | thu-la-kít | ທຸລະກິດ |
| **holiday** | phak phawn | ພັກຜ່ອນ |
| **visiting relatives** | yáam phii-nâwng | ຢາມພີ່ນ້ອງ |
| **visiting the homeland** | yáam bâan kòet | ຢາມບ້ານເກີດ |

## signs

| | |
|---|---|
| ຮ້ອນ | **HOT** |
| ເຢັນ | **COLD** |
| ທາງເຂົ້າ | **ENTRANCE** |
| ທາງອອກ | **EXIT** |
| ເປີດ | **OPEN** |
| ອັດ/ປິດ | **CLOSED** |
| ຫ້າມເຂົ້າ | **NO ENTRY** |
| ຫ້າມສູບຢາ | **NO SMOKING** |
| ຫ້າມ | **PROHIBITED** |
| ຫ້ອງນ້ຳ | **TOILETS** |

## sightseeing

ການທ່ຽວຊົມ

**Where's the tourist office?**
hàwng kạan thawng thiaw yuu săi — ຫ້ອງການທ່ອງທ່ຽວຢູ່ໃສ

**Do you have a local map?**
míi phăen-thii tụa méuang baw — ມີແຜນທີ່ຕົວເມືອງບໍ່

**Do you have a guidebook in English?**
míi pêum nám thiaw pháa săa ạng-kít baw — ມີປຶ້ມນຳທ່ຽວພາສາອັງກິດບໍ່

### what's a wat?

Technically speaking, the wat (ວັດ) is a compound where Buddhist monks and/or nuns reside. In Laos, a typical wat may contain the following structures:

| | | |
|---|---|---|
| **drum tower** | hăw kạwng | ຫໍກອງ |
| **ordination hall** | sĭm | ສິມ |
| **monastic quarters** | kú-tí | ກຸຕິ |
| **stupa** | thâat | ທາດ |

**'bone stupas', where the ashes of worshippers are interred**
thâat ká-dùuk — ທາດກະດູກ

**pavilion, where laity listen to** thám **or Buddhist doctrine**
săa-láa fáng thám — ສາລາຟັງທຳ

**spirit house, for the temple's reigning earth spirit**
hăw phĭi khún wat — ຫໍຜີຄຸນວັດ

**Tipitaka library, where Buddhist scriptures are stored**
hăw tại — ຫໍໄຕ

**What are the main attractions?**
laeng thawng thiaw thii sǎm-khán maen nyǎng — ແຫລ່ງທ່ອງທ່ຽວທີ່ສຳຄັນແມ່ນຫຍັງ

**Can we take photographs?**
thaai hûup dâi baw — ຖ່າຍຮູບໄດ້ບໍ່

**I'll send you the photograph.**
khàwy síi fàak hûup máa hâi — ຂ້ອຍຊິຝາກຮູບມາໃຫ້

**What time does it open/close?**
poet/pít wéh-láa ják móhng — ເປີດ/ປິດເວລາຈັກໂມງ

**Is there an admission charge?**
kép khaa phaan pa-tụu baw — ເກັບຄ່າຜ່ານປະຕູບໍ່

## wat's the story?

Correct behaviour in a wat entails several guidelines, the most important of which is to dress neatly (no shorts or sleeveless shirts) and to take your shoes off when you enter any building that contains a Buddha image. Buddha images are sacred objects, so don't pose in front of them for pictures and definitely do not clamber upon them.

Monks are not supposed to touch or be touched by women. If a woman wants to hand something to a monk, the object should be placed within reach of the monk, not handed directly to him.

When sitting in a religious edifice, keep your feet pointed away from any Buddha images or monks. The usual way to do this is to sit in the 'mermaid' pose in which your legs are folded to the side, with the feet pointing backwards.

| | | |
|---|---|---|
| **Is there a discount for ...?** | lut láa-kháa săm-láp ... baw | ລຸດລາຄາ ສຳລັບ ... ບໍ່ |
| **children** | dék nâwy | ເດັກນ້ອຍ |
| **students** | nak hían | ນັກຮຽນ |

**What's that building?**
nân maen ąa-kháan nyăng — ນັ້ນແມ່ນອາຄານຫຍັງ

**What's this monument?**
nîi maen ąa-nu-săa-wa-líi nyăng — ນີ້ແມ່ນ ອານຸສາວະລີຫຍັງ

**What's that?**
nân maen nyăng — ນັ້ນແມ່ນຫຍັງ

**How old is it?**
ąa-nyu ják pįi lâew — ອາຍຸຈັກປີແລ້ວ

## bargaining

ການຕໍ່ລອງລາຄາ

Negotiating prices, ie, bargaining, is a common practice in Laos, as in most of South-East Asia. You can expect to bargain for most items offered for sale in a market, even when prices are posted. In department stores and convenience shops, however, prices are fixed. Don't go overboard when bargaining – both seller and buyer lose face when you argue too vehemently or haggle over a few kìip (ກີບ).

| | | |
|---|---|---|
| **How much?** | thao dąi | ເທົ່າໃດ |
| **How many kip?** | ják kìip | ຈັກກີບ |

**Do you have something cheaper?**
míi aąn thèuk-kwaa nîi baw — ມີອັນຖືກກ່ວານີ້ບໍ່

**The price is very high.**
láa-kháa pháeng lǎai — ລາຄາແພງຫລາຍ

**I think that's too much.**
khit waa pháeng phôht — ຄິດວ່າແພງໂພດ

**Can you bring the price down?**
lut láa-kháa dâi baw — ລຸດລາຄາໄດ້ບໍ່

**Can you lower it more?**
lut ìik dâi baw — ລຸດອີກໄດ້ບໍ່

**How about ... kip?**
... kìip dâi baw — ... ກີບໄດ້ບໍ່

**I don't have much money.**
khàwy baw míi ngóen lǎai — ຂ້ອຍບໍ່ມີເງິນຫລາຍ

If I/we buy two ... (+ classifier) will you lower the price?
thàa sêu săwng ... lut dâi baw — ຖ້າຊື້ສອງ ... ລຸດໄດ້ບໍ່

The quality is not very good.
khún-na-phâap baw dịi pạan dại — ຄຸນນະພາບບໍ່ດີປານໃດ

What's your lowest price?
láa-kháa tam sút thao dại — ລາຄາຕ່ຳສຸດເທົ່າໃດ

## making a purchase

ການຈັດຊ

| | | |
|---|---|---|
| Do you have any ...? | mịi ... baw | ມີ ... ບໍ່ |
| Please give me ... | khăw ... | ຂໍ ... |
| I'm looking for ... | khàwy sàwk hăa ... | ຂອຍຊອກຫາ ... |
| Do you have any more? | mịi ìik baw | ມີອີກບໍ່ |
| I'd like to see another style. | khăw boeng ìik bàep neung | ຂໍເບິ່ງອີກແບບໜຶ່ງ |
| How much (for) ...? | ... thao dại | ... ເທົ່າໃດ |
| both | tháng săwng | ທັງສອງ |
| per fruit | nuay-la | ໜ່ວຍລະ |
| per metre | maet-la | ແມັດລະ |
| per piece | ạn-la | ອັນລະ |
| this | ạn-nîi | ອັນນີ້ |
| three pieces | săam ạn | ສາມອັນ |

How much altogether?
thuk yaang thao dại — ທຸກຢ່າງເທົ່າໃດ

| | | |
|---|---|---|
| I'd like (a) ... | khàwy tâwng-kạan ... | ຂ້ອຍຕ້ອງການ ... |
| Where can I find (a) ...? | já hăa ... dâi yuu săi | ຈະຫາ ... ໄດ້ຢູ່ໃສ |

PRACTICAL

| | | |
|---|---|---|
| **batteries** | thaan fái săai | ຖ່ານໄຟສາຍ |
| **bread** | khào jii | ເຂົ້າຈີ່ |
| **butter** | bọe | ເບີ |
| **candles** | thían | ທຽນ |
| **cheese** | nóei khăeng | ເນີຍແຂງ |
| **chocolate** | sawk-kọh-laet | ຊັອກໂກແລັດ |
| **eggs** | khai | ໄຂ່ |
| **flour** | pâeng | ແປ້ງ |
| **gas cyclinder** | thăng káet | ຖັງແກສ |
| **ham** | háem | ແຮມ |
| **honey** | nâm phòeng | ນ້ຳເຜີ້ງ |
| **margarine** | mâak-kạa-lín | ມາກກາລີນ |
| **matches** | káp-khìit | ກັບຂີດ |
| **milk** | nâm nóm | ນ້ຳນົມ |
| **mosquito coil** | yạa jùt nyúng | ຢາຈູດຍຸງ |
| **mosquito repellant** | yạa kạn nyúng | ຢາກັ້ນຍຸງ |
| **pepper** | màak phét | ໝາກເຜັດ |
| **salt** | kẹua | ເກືອ |
| **shampoo** | yạa sa hŭa | ຢາຊະຫົວ |
| **soap** | sá-bụu | ສະບູ |
| **sugar** | nâm tạan | ນ້ຳຕານ |
| **toilet paper** | jîa hàwng nâm | ເຈ້ຍຫ້ອງນ້ຳ |
| **toothpaste** | yạa thŭu khàew | ຢາຖູແຂ້ວ |
| **washing powder** | fâep | ແຟບ |

## souvenirs & crafts

ເຄື່ອງທີ່ລະລຶກແລະເຄື່ອງ ຫັດຖະກຳ

Hill-tribe crafts abound in Laos, and make fine souvenirs of your travels. Like elsewhere in South-East Asia, bargaining is a local tradition (originally introduced to the area by early Arab and Indian traders). Although most shops nowadays have fixed prices, fabric, carvings, jewellery and antiques are usually subject to bargaining.

The Lao produce well-crafted carvings in wood, bone and stone. Subjects can be anything from Hindu or Buddhist mythology to themes from everyday life. Opium pipes seem to be plentiful in Laos and sometimes have intricately carved bone or bamboo shafts, along with engraved ceramic bowls. Vientiane, Luang Prabang, Pakse and Savannakhet each have a sprinkling of antique shops. Anything that looks old could be up for sale in these shops, including Asian pottery (especially Ming dynasty porcelain), old jewellery, clothes, carved wood, musical instruments, coins and bronze statuettes.

| | | |
|---|---|---|
| **baskets** | ká-taa | ກະຕ່າ |
| **handicrafts** | kheuang hát-thá-kạm | ເຄື່ອງຫັດຖະກໍາ |
| **pottery/ceramics** | kheuang dìn | ເຄື່ອງດິນ |

## materials

ວັດຖຸ

| | | |
|---|---|---|
| **What is this made of?** | nîi het dûay nyăng | ນີ້ເຮັດດ້ວຍຫຍັງ |
| **aluminium** | áa-lúu-míi-níam | ອາລູມີນຽມ |
| **brass** | tháwng lĕuang | ທອງເຫລືອງ |
| **bronze** | tháwng săm-lit | ທອງສໍາລິດ |
| **cloth** | phàa | ຜ້າ |
| **copper** | tháwng dạeng | ທອງແດງ |
| **gold (pure)** | khám | ຄໍາ |
| **gold-plated** | khám bại | ຄໍາໃບ |
| **leather** | năng | ໜັງ |
| **silver** | ngóen | ເງິນ |
| **stone** | hĭn | ຫີນ |
| **teak** | mâi sák | ໄມ້ສັກ |
| **wood** | mâi | ໄມ້ |

PRACTICAL

## lao looms

All together Laos is said to have some 16 basic weaving styles divided among four basic regions. Southern weavers, who often use foot looms rather than frame looms, practise Laos' most continuous textile traditions in terms of styles and patterns, some of which haven't changed for a century or more. Southern Laos is known for the best silk weaving and for intricate mat-mịi (ikat or tie-dye) designs that include Khmer-influenced temple and elephant motifs. Synthetic and natural dyes are commonly used.

In north-eastern Laos (especially Hua Phan's Sam Neua and Xieng Khuang's Muang Phuan) the Thai Neua, Phuan, Thai Lü, Thai Daeng, Thai Dam and Phu Thai mainly produce weft brocade (yìap ko) using raw silk, cotton yarn and natural dyes, sometimes with the addition of mat-mịi techniques. Large diamond patterns are common.

In central Laos, typical weavings include indigo-dyed cotton mat-míi and minimal weft brocade (jók and khít), along with techniques borrowed from all over the country (brought by migrants to Vientiane – many of whom fled war zones). Gold and silver brocade is typical of traditional Luang Prabang patterns, along with intricate patterns (lái) and imported Thai Lü designs.

Northerners generally use frame looms; the waist, body and bottom border of a phàa nung or sarong are often sewn together from separately woven pieces.

# textiles

ຜ້າແພ

| | | |
|---|---|---|
| **cotton** | phàa fàai | ຜ້າຝ້າຍ |
| **embroidery** | phàa thák saew | ຜ້າຫັກແສ່ວ |
| **ikat-style tie-dyed cloth** | mat-mii | ມັດໝີ |
| **minimal weft brocade** | jók/khít | ຈົກ/ຂິດ |

| | | |
|---|---|---|
| **silk** | phàa mǎi | ຜ້າໄໝ |
| **shoulder bag** | thǒng pháai | ຖົງພາຍ |
| **traditional long sarong for women** | sìin | ສິ້ນ |

## gems & jewellery

ເພັດພອຍ ແລະ ເຄື່ອງປະດັບ

Gold and silver jewellery is a good buy in Laos, although you must search hard for well-made pieces. Some of the best silverwork is done by the hill tribes. Gems are also sometimes available, but you can get better prices in Thailand.

Most provincial towns have a few shops that specialise in jewellery. You can also find jewellery in antique and handicraft shops.

| | | |
|---|---|---|
| **bracelet** | sǎi khǎen | ສາຍແຂນ |
| **diamond** | phet | ເພັດ |
| **emerald** | kâew máw-la-kót | ແກ້ວມໍລະກົດ |
| **gems** | phet pháwy | ເພັດພອຍ |
| **jade** | nyók | ຫຍົກ |
| **necklace** | sǎai kháw | ສາຍຄໍ |
| **ring** | wǎen | ແຫວນ |
| **ruby** | thap thím | ທັບທິມ |
| **sapphire** | pháwy sǐi kháam | ພອຍສີຄາມ |
| **silver** | ngóen | ເງິນ |

PRACTICAL

## clothing

ເຄື່ອງ

The general Lao word for clothing is sèua phàa (ເສື້ອຜ້າ). Sèua (ເສື້ອ) itself can mean 'shirt', 'blouse', 'dress' or 'jacket'; phàa (ຜ້າ) means 'cloth'.

| | | |
|---|---|---|
| **hat** | mùak | ໝວກ |
| **shirt/blouse/ jacket/dress** | sèua | ເສື້ອ |
| **shoes** | kòep | ເກີບ |
| **skirt (Lao-style)** | sìin | ສິ້ນ |
| **skirt (Western-style)** | ká-pohng | ກະໂປ່ງ |
| **socks** | thŏng thâo | ຖົງເທົ້າ |
| **style** | bàep | ແບບ |
| **tailor** | saang tát kheuang | ຊ່າງຕັດເຄື່ອງ |
| **trousers** | sòng khăa nyáo | ສົ້ງຂາຍາວ |
| **underwear** | sòng sâwn | ສົ້ງຊ້ອນ |
| **Can you make ...?** | tát ... dâi baw | ຕັດ ... ໄດ້ບໍ່ |
| **The sleeves are too ...** | khăen ... phôht | ແຂນ ... ໂພດ |
| **long** | nyáo | ຍາວ |
| **short** | sàn | ສັ້ນ |

shopping

## fabrics

ຜ້າ

Synthetic materials and Western fabric weaves use the same names as in English (eg, polyester, dacron, serge, gabardine, etc), spoken with a Lao accent.

| | | |
|---|---|---|
| **cotton** | phàa fàai | ຜ້າຝ້າຍ |
| **leather** | năng | ໜັງ |
| **linen** | phàa lîi-nín | ຜ້າລີນິນ |
| **silk** | phàa măi | ຜ້າໄໝ |
| **wool** | phàa khŏn sát | ຜ້າຂົນສັດ |

PRACTICAL

## colours

ສີ

| | | |
|---|---|---|
| dark | sǐi kae | ສີແກ່ |
| light | sǐi awn | ສີອ່ອນ |
| black | sǐi dạm | ສີດຳ |
| blue | sǐi fâa | ສີຟ້າ |
| brown | sǐi nâm-tạan | ສີນ້ຳຕານ |
| green | sǐi khǐaw | ສີຂຽວ |
| grey | sǐi khìi thao | ສີຂີ້ເທົາ |
| pink | sǐi bụa | ສີບົວ |
| purple | sǐi muang | ສີມ່ວງ |
| red | sǐi dạeng | ສີແດງ |
| white | sǐi khǎo | ສີຂາວ |
| yellow | sǐi lěuang | ສີເຫລືອງ |

**Do you have another colour?**
míi sǐi eun baw — ມີສີອື່ນບໍ່

## toiletries

ເຄື່ອງສຳອາງ

| | | |
|---|---|---|
| brush | pạeng | ແປງ |
| comb | wǐi | ຫວີ |
| condoms | thǒng yạang á-náa-mái | ຖົງຢາງອະນາໄມ |
| dental floss | sêuak jìim khàew | ເຊືອກຈີ້ມແຂ້ວ |
| deodorant | yạa kạn kin tụa | ຢາກັນກິນຕົວ |
| moisturiser | khíim tháa nàa | ຄີມທາໜ້າ |
| razor | mîit thǎe | ມີດແຖ |
| razor blades | bại mîit thǎe | ໃບມີດແຖ |
| sanitary napkins | phàa á-náa-mái | ຜ້າອະນາໄມ |
| shampoo | nâm yạa sá phǒm | ນ້ຳຢາຊະຜົມ |
| shaving cream | yáa thǎe nùat | ຢາແຖໜວດ |
| soap | sá-bụu | ສະບູ |
| sunblock | yáa kạn dàet | ຢາກັນແດດ |
| tissues | jîa á-náa-mái | ເຈ້ຍອະນາໄມ |
| toilet paper | jîa hàwng nâm | ເຈ້ຍຫ້ອງນ້ຳ |
| toothbrush | pạeng thǔu khàew | ແປງຖູແຂ້ວ |
| toothpaste | yạa thǔu khàew | ຢາຖູແຂ້ວ |

## stationery & publications

ເຈ້ຍແລະສິ່ງພິມ

| | | |
|---|---|---|
| **book** | pêum | ປຶ້ມ |
| **bookshop** | hàan khǎai pêum | ຮ້ານຂາຍປຶ້ມ |
| **envelope** | sáwng jót-mǎai | ຊອງຈົດໝາຍ |
| **guidebook** | pêum thawng thiaw | ປຶ້ມທ່ອງທ່ຽວ |
| **ink** | nâm móek | ນ້ຳເມິກ |
| **magazine** | wáa-la-sǎan | ວາລະສານ |
| **newspaper** | nǎng-sěu phím | ໜັງສືພິມ |
| **notebook** | pêum bạn théuk | ປຶ້ມບັນທຶກ |
| **pen** | bík | ບິກ |
| **pencil** | sǎw dạm | ສໍດຳ |
| **stationery** | keuang khǐan | ເຄື່ອງຂຽນ |
| **writing paper** | jîa khǐan | ເຈ້ຍຂຽນ |

## photography

ການຖ່າຍຮູບ

| | | |
|---|---|---|
| **camera** | kâwng thaai hûup | ກ້ອງຖ່າຍຮູບ |
| **develop (photos)** | lâang hûup | ລ້າງຮູບ |
| **lens** | léhn | ເລນ |
| **photograph** | hûup | ຮູບ |
| **to photograph** | thaai hûup | ຖາຍຮູບ |
| **film** | fím hûup | ຟິມຮູບ |
| **colour** | fím sǐi | ຟິມສີ |
| **B&W** | fím khǎo dạm | ຟິມຂາວດຳ |
| **slide film** | fím sá-lái | ຟິມສະໄລ |

**When will it be ready?**
wéh-láa-dại já lâang hûup jóp lâew — ເວລາໃດຈະລ້າງຮູບຈົບແລ້ວ

**How many days?**
ják mêu — ຈັກມື້

PRACTICAL

## smoking

ສູບຢາ

**A packet of ... cigarettes, please.**
ąo yąa sùup hài dae sáwng nèung — ເອົາຢາສູບໃຫ້ແດ່ຊອງໜຶ່ງ

**Are these cigarettes strong or mild?**
yąa nîi púk lĕu jąang — ຢານີ້ປຸກຫລືຈາງ

**Do you have a light?**
míi káp fái baw — ມີກັບໄຟບໍ່

**Please don't smoke.**
ká-lu-náa yąa sùup yáa — ກະລຸນາຢ່າສູບຢາ

**Can I smoke?**
sùup yąa dâi baw — ສູບຢາໄດ້ບໍ່

| | | |
|---|---|---|
| cigarettes | yąa sùup | ຢາສູບ |
| cigarette papers | jîa phán yąa sùup | ເຈັ້ຍພັນຢາສູບ |
| filtered | kąwng | ກອງ |
| lighter | káp fái | ກັບໄຟ |
| matches | káp khìit | ກັບຂີດ |
| menthol | yáa sùup yén | ຢາສູບເຢັນ |
| pipe | kàwk | ກອກ |
| tobacco | yáa sèn | ຢາເສັ້ນ |

## weights & measures

ການຊັ່ງແລະການວັດແທກ

Dimensions and weight are usually expressed using the metric system in Laos. The exception is land measure, which is usually quoted using the traditional system of wáa, ngáan and hâi. Gold jewellery is often measured in baht (bàat).

### one loh of bread

Don't forget to use a classifier when indicating a number of something – the general-purpose classifier that should get you through is loh. Find more classifiers on page 40.

| | | |
|---|---|---|
| 1 wáa | = 4 sq metres | ວາ |
| 1 ngáan (100 sq wáa) | = 400 sq metres | ງານ |
| 1 hâi (4 ngáan) | = 1600 sq metres | ໄຮ່ |
| 1 bàat | = 15 grams | ບາດ |
| kilogram | kí-lóh | ກິໂລ |
| kilometre | kí-lóh-maet | ກິໂລແມັດ |
| metre | maet | ແມັດ |
| litre | liit | ລິດ |

## sizes & comparisons

ຂະໜາດແລະການສົມທຽບ

| | | |
|---|---|---|
| Do you have anything ... than this? | míi ... nîi baw | ມີ ... ນີ້ບໍ່ |
| larger | nyai-kwaa | ໃຫຍ່ກ່ວາ |
| smaller | nâwy-kwaa | ນ້ອຍກ່ວາ |
| too tight | kháp phôht | ຄັບໂພດ |
| too small | nâwy phôht | ນ້ອຍໂພດ |
| too large | nyai phôht | ໃຫຍ່ໂພດ |
| too wide | kwâang phôht | ກ້ວາງໂພດ |
| too long | nyáo phôht | ຍາວໂພດ |
| too short | sàn phôht | ສັ້ນໂພດ |
| to bargain | taw | ຕໍ່ |
| to buy | sêu | ຊື້ |
| cheap | thèuk | ຖືກ |
| expensive | pháeng | ແພງ |
| quality | khún-na-phâap | ຄຸນນະພາບ |
| sell | khǎai | ຂາຍ |
| size | kha-nàat | ຂະໜາດ |
| not enough | baw pháw | ບໍ່ພໍ |
| good enough | pháw dịi | ພໍດີ |
| I'd like to see ... | yàak boeng ... | ຢາກເບິ່ງ ... |
| this one | ạn nîi | ອັນນີ້ |
| that one | ạn nân | ອັນນັ້ນ |
| Which one? | ạn dại | ອັນໃດ |
| Do you have any more? | míi iik baw | ມີອີກບໍ່ |

PRACTICAL

## disabled travellers

ນັກທ່ອງທ່ຽວພິການ

**I'm disabled.**
khàwy pẹn khón phi-kạan — ຂ້ອຍເປັນຄົນພິການ

**I need assistance.**
khàwy tâwng-kạan khwáam suay lĕua — ຂ້ອຍຕ້ອງການຄວາມຊ່ວຍເຫລືອ

**What services do you have for disabled people?**
jâo bạw-li-kạan nyăng dae săm-láp khón phi-kạan — ເຈົ້າບໍລິການຫຍັງແດ່ສຳລັບຄົນພິການ

**Is there wheelchair access?**
kạo-îi lâw kháo pại dâi baw — ເກົ້າອີ້ລໍ້ເຂົ້າໄປໄດ້ບໍ່

**Can you bring me a wheelchair?**
jâo ạo kạo-îi lâw máa hap khàwy dâi baw — ເຈົ້າເອົາເກົ້າອີ້ລໍ້ມາຮັບຂ້ອຍໄດ້ບໍ່

**I'm deaf.**
khàwy hŭu nùak — ຂ້ອຍຫູໜວກ

**I have a hearing aid.**
khàwy míi kheuang suay fáng — ຂ້ອຍມີເຄື່ອງຊ່ວຍຟັງ

**Speak more loudly, please.**
ká-lu-náa wâo dạng-dạng dae — ກະລຸນາເວົ້າດັງໆແດ່

**Are guide dogs permitted?**
măa suay khon tạa bàwt á-nu-nyâat baw — ໝາຊ່ວຍຄົນຕາບອດອະນຸຍາດບໍ່

**disabled person**
khón phi-kạan — ຄົນພິການ

**guide dog**
măa suay khón tạa bàwt — ໝາຊ່ວຍຄົນຕາບອດ

**wheelchair**
kạo îi lâw — ເກົ້າອີ້ລໍ້

# travelling with the family

ເດີນທາງກັບຄອບຄົວ

**Are there facilities for babies?**
mı́i sing ąm-núay khwáam sá-dùak sǎm-láp dék baw
ມີສິ່ງອຳນວຍຄວາມ ສະດວກສຳລັບເດັກບໍ່

**Do you have a child-minding service?**
mı́i bąw-li-kąan dųu láe dék nâwy baw
ມີບໍລິການດູ ແລເດັກນ້ອຍບໍ່

**Where can I find a ... -speaking babysitter? [insert country name from page 116]**
khàwy já hǎa khón lîang dék thii hûu pháa-sǎa ... dâi yuu sǎi
ຂ້ອຍຈະຫາຄົນລ້ຽງ ເດັກທີ່ຮູ້ພາສາ ... ໄດ້ຢູ່ໃສ

**Can you put an extra bed/cot in the room?**
suay sǒem tįang nái hàwng hài dae dâi baw
ຊ່ວຍເສີມຕຽງ ໃນຫ້ອງໃຫ້ແດ່ໄດ້ບໍ່

**I need a car with a child seat.**
khàwy tâwng-kąan lot thii mı́i bawn nâng sǎm-láp dék nâwy
ຂ້ອຍຕ້ອງການລົດທີ່ມີ ບ່ອນນັ່ງສຳລັບເດັກນ້ອຍ

**Is it suitable for children?**
mán máw-sǒm sǎm-láp dèk nâwy baw
ມັນເໝາະສົມສຳລັບ ເດັກນ້ອຍບໍ່

**Is there a family discount?**
mı́i suan lut láa-kháa sǎm-láp khâwp khúa baw
ມີສ່ວນລຸດລາຄາ ສຳລັບຄອບຄົວບໍ່

**Do you have a children's menu?**
mı́i láai-kąan ąa-hǎan dék nâwy baw
ມີລາຍການອາຫານ ເດັກນ້ອຍບໍ່

**Are there any activities for children?**
mı́i kít-já-kąm sǎm-láp dék nâwy baw
ມີກິດຈະກຳສຳລັບ ເດັກນ້ອຍບໍ່

## looking for a job

ການຊອກຫາງານທຳ

**Where can I find local job advertisements?**
khàwy já sâwk hǎa pá-kàat hap sá-mak ngáan khó-sá-náa dâi yuu sǎi
ຂ້ອຍຈະຊອກຫາ ປະກາດຮັບສະມັກງານ ໂຄສະນາໄດ້ຢູ່ໃສ

**Do I need a work permit?**
khàwy tâwng-kạan míi bại á-nu-nyâat het wîak baw
ຂ້ອຍຕ້ອງການມີໃບ ອະນຸຍາດເຮັດວຽກບໍ່

**I've had experience.**
khàwy míi pá-sóp-kạan
ຂ້ອຍມີປະສົບການ

**I've come about the position advertised.**
khàwy máa pheua tạm-naeng thii dâi khó-sá-náa
ຂ້ອຍມາເພື່ອຕຳແໜ່ງ ທີ່ໄດ້ໂຄສະນາ

**I'm ringing about the position advertised.**
khàwy thóh máa kiaw-káp tạm-naeng thii dâi khó-sá-náa
ຂ້ອຍໂທມາກ່ຽວກັບ ຕຳແໜ່ງທີ່ໄດ້ໂຄສະນາ

**What's the wage?**
ngóen dẹuan thao dại
ເງິນເດືອນເທົ່າໃດ

**Do I have to pay tax?**
khàwy tâwng sǐa pháa-sǐi baw
ຂ້ອຍຕ້ອງເສຍພາສີບໍ່

**I can start ...**
khàwy sǎa-mâat loem ...
ຂ້ອຍສາມາດ ເລີ່ມ

| | | |
|---|---|---|
| today | mêu nîi | ມື້ນີ້ |
| tomorrow | mêu eun | ມື້ອື່ນ |
| next week | ạa-thit nàa | ອາທິດໜ້າ |

## useful words

ຄຳສັບທີ່ເປັນປະໂຫຍດ

| | | |
|---|---|---|
| casual | thám-ma-dąa | ທຳມະດາ |
| employee | lûuk jâang | ລູກຈ້າງ |
| employer | náai jâang | ນາຍຈ້າງ |
| full-time | tęm wéh-láa | ເຕັມເວລາ |
| job | wîak | ວຽກ |
| occupation/trade | ąa-sîip | ອາຊີບ |
| part-time | khoeng wéh-láa | ເຄິ່ງເວລາ |
| resume/cv | síi-wa pá-wat yàw | ຊີວະປະຫວັດຫຍໍ້ |
| traineeship | théun kąan féuk óp-hóm | ທຶນການຝຶກອົບຮົມ |
| work experience | pá-sóp-kąan het wîak | ປະສົບການເຮັດວຽກ |

## on business

ດຳເນີນທຸລະກິດ

| | | |
|---|---|---|
| We're attending a ... | phûak háo khào huam ... | ພວກເຮົາ ເຂົ້າຮ່ວມ ... |
| conference | kąwng pá-súm sǎm-ma-náa | ກອງປະຊຸມ ສຳມະນາ |
| meeting | pá-súm | ປະຊຸມ |
| trade fair | ngáan wáang sá-dąeng sǐn khâa | ງານວາງ ສະແດງສິນຄ້າ |
| workshop/ seminar | sǎm-ma-náa | ສຳມະນາ |

PRACTICAL

**I'm on a course.**
khàwy kạm-láng hían — ຂ້ອຍກຳລັງຮຽນ

**I have an appointment with ...**
khàwy míi nat káp ... — ຂ້ອຍມີນັດກັບ ...

**Here's my business card.**
nîi maen bát thu-la-kít khǎwng khàwy — ນີ້ແມ່ນບັດທຸລະກິດຂອງຂ້ອຍ

**I need an interpreter.**
khàwy tâwng-kạan phùu pạe pháa-sǎa — ຂ້ອຍຕ້ອງການຜູ້ແປພາສາ

**I'd like to use a computer.**
khàwy yàak sâi kháwm-pịi-tọe — ຂ້ອຍຢາກໃຊ້ຄອມປິເຕີ

**I'd like to send [a fax; an email].**
khàwy yàak song fáek/ịi-máew — ຂ້ອຍຢາກສົ່ງແຟກ/ອີແມວ

## useful words

ຄຳສັບທີ່ເປັນປະໂຫຍດ

| | | |
|---|---|---|
| mobile phone | thóh-la-sáp méu thěu | ໂທລະສັບມືຖື |
| client | lûuk khâa | ລູກຄ້າ |
| colleague | pheuan huam ngáan | ເພື່ອນຮ່ວມງານ |
| distributor | phùu jạm-naai | ຜູ້ຈັດຈຳໜ່າຍ |
| email | ịi-máew | ອີແມວ |
| exhibition | ngáan wáang sá-dạeng | ງານວາງສະແດງ |
| manager | phùu ját kạan | ຜູ້ຈັດການ |
| profit | kạm-lái | ກຳໄລ |
| proposal | khàw sá-nǒe | ຂໍສະເໜີ |

## on tour

ມາທ່ອງທ່ຽວ

**We're part of a group.**
phûak háo maen ká-lup — ພວກເຮົາແມ່ນກະລຸບ

**We're on tour.**
phûak háo het thúa — ພວກເຮົາເຮັດທົວ

| I'm with the ... | máa káp ... | ມາກັບ ... |
|---|---|---|
| group | ká-lup | ກະລຸບ |
| band | wóng dọn-tịi | ວົງດົນຕີ |
| team | kha-na phùu lìn | ຄະນະຜູ້ຫລິ້ນ |
| crew | phûak lûuk méu | ພວກລູກມື |

**Please speak with our manager.**
ká-lu-náa lóm káp phùu ját kạan phûak háo — ກະລຸນາລົມກັບຜູ້ຈັດການພວກເຮົາ

**We've lost our equipment.**
phûak háo het kheuang ú-pá-kạwn sïa — ພວກເຮົາເຮັດເຄື່ອງອຸປະກອນເສຍ

| We sent equipment on this ... | phûak háo song kheuang ú-pá-kạwn tháang ... | ພວກເຮົາສົ່ງເຄື່ອງອຸປະກອນທາງ ... |
|---|---|---|
| flight | thìaw bịn | ຖ້ຽວບິນ |
| bus | lot méh | ລົດເມ |

**We're taking a break of ... days.**
phûak háo phak kạan ... mêu — ພວກເຮົາພັກການ ... ມື້

**We're playing on ...**
phûak háo já lìn ... — ພວກເຮົາຈະຫລິ້ນ ...

**did you know ...**

Buddhism is practised by approximately 60% of the Lao population; animism and other religions make up the remainder.

PRACTICAL

## film & tv crews

ຄະນະຖ່າຍທຳແລະ ຄະນະຖ່າຍທຳໂທລະພາບ

We're on location.
phûak háo yuu thii sá-thăan thii thaai thám
ພວກເຮົາຢູ່ທີ່ສະຖານທີ່ຖ່າຍທຳ

We're filming!
kąam-láng thaai thám
ກຳລັງຖ່າຍທຳ

May we film here?
thaai thám yuu nîi dâi baw
ຖ່າຍທຳຢູ່ນີ້ໄດ້ບໍ່

| We're making a ... | phûak háo thaai ... | ພວກເຮົາຖ່າຍ ... |
|---|---|---|
| documentary | fím èhk-á-săan | ຟີມເອກະສານ |
| film | năng leuang | ໜັງເລື່ອງ |
| TV series | tąwn thóh-la-thát | ຕອນໂທລະທັດ |

## pilgrimage & religion

ການເຄົາລົບບູຊາແລະສາສະນາ

| I'm ... | khàwy thĕu ... | ຂ້ອຍຖື ... |
|---|---|---|
| Buddhist | sàat-sá-náa phut | ສາສະນາພຸດ |
| Christian | sàat-sá-náa khlit | ສາສະນາຄຣິດ |
| Hindu | sàat-sá-náa hín-dųu | ສາສະນາຮິນດູ |
| Jewish | sàat-sá-náa yíu | ສາສະນາຢິວ |
| Muslim | sàat-sá-náa mu-sá-lím | ສາສະນາມຸສລິມ |

I'm not religious.
khàwy baw thĕu sàat-sá-náa
ຂ້ອຍບໍ່ຖືສາສະນາ

I'm (Catholic), but not practising.
khàwy maen (kąa-tọh-lik) tae baw dâi thĕu
ຂ້ອຍແມ່ນ (ກາໂຕລິກ) ແຕ່ບໍ່ໄດ້ນັບຖື

specific needs

**I think I believe in God.**
khit waa seua thěu pha-phùu pẹn jâo — ຄິດວ່າເຊື່ອຖືພະຜູ້ເປັນເຈົ້າ

**I believe in destiny.**
khàwy seua thěu sá-tạa-kạm — ຂ້ອຍເຊື່ອຖືສະຕາກັມ

**I'm interested in astrology/ philosophy.**
khàwy sŏn jại hŏ-la-sàat/pát-sá-yáa — ຂ້ອຍສົນໃຈໂຫລະສາດ/ ປັດສະຍາ

**I'm an atheist.**
khàwy baw seua thěu pha-phùu pẹn jâo — ຂ້ອຍບໍ່ເຊື່ອຖືພະຜູ້ ເປັນເຈົ້າ

**I'm agnostic.**
khàwy seua thěu thám-ma-dàa — ຂ້ອຍເຊື່ອຖືທຳມະດາ

**Can I attend this ceremony?**
khàwy săa-mâat khào huam phi-thíi nîi dâi baw — ຂ້ອຍສາມາດເຂົ້າຮ່ວມ ພິທີນີ້ໄດ້ບໍ່

**Can I pray here?**
sùut món yuu nîi dâi baw — ສູດມົນຢູ່ນີ້ໄດ້ບໍ່

**Where can I pray?**
khàwy săa-mâat sùut món dâi yuu săi — ຂ້ອຍສາມາດສູດມົນ ໄດ້ຢູ່ໃສ

| | | |
|---|---|---|
| **Buddhist temple; monastery** | wat | ວັດ |
| **church** | bòht khlit | ໂບດຄລິດ |
| **funeral** | ngáan sáa-pạa-na-kít sóp | ງານ ຊາປານະກິດຊົບ |

### a little in us all ...

The traditional religion of Laos is animism – the belief that a soul or spirit can be found in all objects, animate or inanimate. Practice of these beliefs can still be seen today at Wat Si Muang in Vientiene. Here, the central image of the temple is the city pillar, where the city's guardian spirit is said to reside.

| | | |
|---|---|---|
| god | pha jâo | ພະເຈົ້າ |
| monk | khuu-bạa, nak bùat | ຄູບາ ນັກບວດ |
| prayer | kạan sùut món | ການສູດມົນ |
| priest | khún phaw (nái sàat-sá-náa khlit) | ຄຸນພໍ່ (ໃນສາສະນາຄລິດ) |
| religious ceremony | phi-thíi kạm sàat-sá-náa | ພິທີກຳສາສະນາ |
| sabbath | wán sǐn | ວັນສິນ |
| saint | khón jại pha | ຄົນໃຈພະ |
| shrine | hǎw wài | ຫໍໄຫວ້ |
| stupa | thâat | ທາດ |

## tracing roots & history

ຊອກຄົ້ນຫາ ບັນພະບູລຸດ ແລະ ປະຫວັດສາດ

**I think my ancestors came from this area.**
khit waa bạn-pha-bụu-lút khǎwng khàwy máa jàak bạw-li-wéhn nîi
ຄິດວ່າບັນພະບູລຸດຂອງຂ້ອຍມາຈາກບໍລິເວນນີ້

**I'm looking for my relatives.**
khàwy sâwk hǎa phii-nâwng khǎwng khàwy
ຂ້ອຍຊອກຫາພີ່ນ້ອງຂອງຂ້ອຍ

**I have a relative who lives around here.**
khàwy míi phii-nâwng yuu thii nîi
ຂ້ອຍມີພີ່ນ້ອງຢູ່ທີ່ນີ້

specific needs

**Is there anyone here by the name of ...?**
yuu nîi míi khón seu ... ຢູ່ນີ້ມີຄົນຊື່

**I'd like to go to the burial ground.**
khàwy yàak pại bawn făng sóp ຂ້ອຍຢາກໄປບ່ອນຝັງຊົບ

**My (father) was stationed here during the Indochina War.**
nái pạang sŏng-kháam ịn-dụu-jịin phaw khăwng khàwy dâi pá-jạm yuu thii nîi ໃນປາງສົງຄາມອິນດູຈີນ ພໍ່ຂອງຂ້ອຍໄດ້ ປະຈໍາຢູ່ທີ່ນີ້

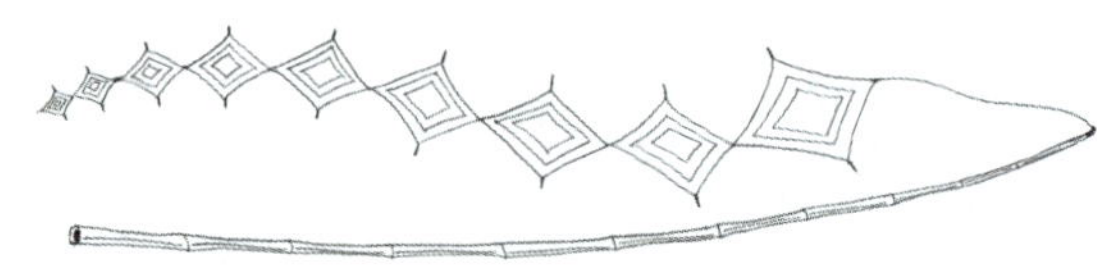

PRACTICAL

The all-purpose Lao greeting (and farewell) is sá-bąai-dįi (ສະບາຍດີ). It's often accompanied by a nop (ນົບ), the palms-together gesture of respect, or by a light handshake. If someone says sá-bąai-dįi to you, you should reply with the same phrase. A smile and sá-bąai-dįi goes a long way toward calming the initial trepidation that locals may feel upon seeing a foreigner, whether in the city or the countryside.

## you should know

ໜ້າຈະຮູ້

| | | |
|---|---|---|
| **How are you?** | sá-bąai-dįi baw | ສະບາຍດີບໍ່ |
| **I'm fine.** | sá-bąai-dįi | ສະບາຍດີ |
| **Thank you.** | khàwp jąi | ຂອບໃຈ |
| **And you?** | jâo dęh | ເຈົ້າເດ |
| **Thank you very much.** | khàwp jąi lăi lăi | ຂອບໃຈຫລາຍໆ |
| **It's nothing. (never mind; don't bother)** | baw pęn nyăng | ບໍ່ເປັນຫຍັງ |
| **Excuse me.** | khăw thôht | ຂໍໂທດ |

### it's all in the hands

Traditionally the Lao greet each other not with a handshake but with a prayer-like, palms-together gesture known as a nop (ນົບ). If someone nop-s you, you should nop back (unless nop-ed by a child). In Vientiane and large cities, a light version of the Western-style handshake is commonly offered to foreigners.

To beckon someone to come towards you, wave your hand with the palm down. This same gesture can be used to hail public transport along the side of the road.

A quick lifting of the eyebrows is often used to express affirmation or consent.

## greetings

ການທັກທາຍ

As well as sá-bąai-dįi, other common greetings – especially when meeting someone on the road – are pąi sǎį (ໄປໃສ, 'Where are you going?') and kįn khào lâew baw (ກິນເຂົ້າແລ້ວບໍ່, 'Have you eaten yet?'). As with the English 'How are you?', the answer doesn't usually matter. If you're just out for a stroll, a common reply to pąi sǎi is nyaang lín (ຍ່າງຫລິ້ນ), which roughly translates into 'I'm just walking for fun'.

The greeting kin kháo lâew baw carries an implicit invitation to dine together (even for just a quick bowl of noodles), hence you choose the reply based on whether you'd like to spend time with the greeter. Answer nyáng (ຍັງ, 'Not yet') if you're willing to accept a possible meal invitation; answer kin lâew (ກິນແລ້ວ, 'I've eaten already'), if you'd rather be on your way.

## goodbyes

ລາກ່ອນ

As mentioned, a simple sá-bąai-dįi can be used as a farewell, especially if both speakers are leaving at the same time.

If you are leaving and the person you're speaking to is staying behind, you can say láa kawn (ລາກ່ອນ, 'leaving first') or pąi káwn (ໄປກ່ອນ, 'going first'). If you're the one staying, you bid farewell by saying sôhk dįi (ໂຊກດີ, 'good luck').

Whether you're staying or going, it can also be appropriate to say phop kąn mai (ພົບກັນໃໝ່), meaning 'We'll meet again' (roughly equivalent to 'See you later').

## forms of address

ການຮຽກເອີ້ນ

The Lao generally address each other using their first names with a kinship term or other title preceding it. Other formal terms of address include thaan (ທ່ານ, Mr) and náang (ນາງ, Miss

SOCIAL

or Mrs). Friends often use nicknames or kinship terms like âai/ êuay (elder brother/sister), nâwng (younger sibling) or lúng/pâa (uncle/aunt) depending on the age differential. Young children can be called lǎan (nephew or niece).

The following list includes kinship terms commonly used as forms of address for non-family members, based on relative age difference from the speaker. For more kinship terms, see Family on page 118.

| | | |
|---|---|---|
| **elder sister** | êuay | ເອື້ອຍ |
| **elder brother** | âai | ອ້າຍ |
| **younger sibling** | nâwng | ນ້ອງ |
| **grandmother** | mae thào | ແມ່ເຖົ້າ |
| **grandfather** | phaw thào | ພໍ່ເຖົ້າ |
| **aunt** | pâa | ປ້າ |
| **uncle** | lúng | ລຸງ |
| **niece/nephew** | lǎan | ຫລານ |

## body language

ພາສາໃບ້

Non-verbal behaviour is very important in Laos, perhaps more important than in most Western countries.

When walking indoors in front of someone who's sitting down, you should stoop a little as a sign of respect.

### sin-ful

Wearing clothes that bare the thighs, shoulders or breasts is often perceived as improper or disrespectful behaviour in Laos. Long trousers and walking shorts for men and women, as well as skirts, are acceptable attire. Tank tops, sleeveless blouses and short skirts or shorts are not. Many visiting women find that the traditional Lao sìn, a long patterned skirt, makes fine travel wear. For Lao women, such dress is mandatory for visits to government offices and museums.

The feet are the lowest part of the body (spiritually as well as physically) so don't point your feet at people or point at things with your feet. In the same context, the head is regarded as the highest part of the body, so don't touch the Lao on the head either.

## first encounters

ການປະເສີນໜ້າຄັ້ງທຳອິດ

| | |
|---|---|
| **What's your name?** <br> jâo seu nyăng | ເຈົ້າຊື່ຫຍັງ |
| **My name is ...** <br> khàwy seu ... | ຂ້ອຍຊື່ ... |
| **Glad to know you.** <br> nyín dį thii dâi hûu-ják | ຍິນດີທີ່ໄດ້ຮູ້ຈັກ |

## making conversation

ການສົນທະນາ

| | |
|---|---|
| **We're friends.** <br> háo pęn pheuan kąn | ເຮົາເປັນເພື່ອນກັນ |
| **We're relatives.** <br> háo pęn phii-nâwng kąn | ເຮົາເປັນພີ່ນ້ອງກັນ |
| **I've come on business.** <br> khàwy máa het thu-la-kít | ຂ້ອຍມາເຮັດທຸລະກິດ |
| **I've come on pleasure.** <br> khàwy máa thîaw | ຂ້ອຍມາທ່ຽວ |
| **Nice weather, isn't it?** <br> aa-káat dį maen baw | ອາກາດດີແມ່ນບໍ່ |
| **It's quite hot in Laos.** <br> meúang láo hâwn lăai | ເມືອງລາວຮ້ອນຫລາຍ |
| **I like it here.** <br> khàwy mak yuu nîi | ຂ້ອຍມັກຢູ່ນີ້ |
| **May I have your address?** <br> khăw thii-yuu khăwng jâo dâi baw | ຂໍທີ່ຢູ່ຂອງເຈົ້າໄດ້ບໍ່ |

**This is my address.**
nîi maen thii-yuu khǎwng khàwy — ນີ້ແມ່ນທີ່ຢູ່ຂອງຂ້ອຍ

| | | |
|---|---|---|
| **address** | thii-yuu | ທີ່ຢູ່ |
| **fluent** | lian lǎai | ຫລ່ຽນໄຫລ |
| **friend** | pheuan | ເພື່ອນ |
| **language** | pháa-sǎa | ພາສາ |
| **phone number** | nám-bọe thóh-la-sáp | ນຳເບີ້ໂທລະສັບ |
| **study/learn** | hían | ຮຽນ |

## breaking the language barrier

ຄວາມຫຍຸ້ງຍາກດ້ານພາສາ

**I can't speak (much) Lao.**
khàwy pàak pháa-sǎa láo baw dâi (lǎai) — ຊ້ອຍປາກພາສາລາວ ບໍ່ໄດ້(ຫລາຍ)

**I can't speak Lao well.**
khàwy pàak pháa-sǎa láo baw keng — ຊ້ອຍປາກພາສາລາວ ບໍ່ເກັ່ງ

**Can you speak English?**
jâo pàak pháa-sǎa ạng-kít dâi baw — ເຈົ້າປາກພາສາອັງກິດໄດ້ບໍ່

**A little.**
náwy neung — ໜ້ອຍໜຶ່ງ

**I speak ... [insert country name from page 116]**
khàwy pàak pháa-sǎa ... — ຂ້ອຍປາກພາສາ ...

**Please speak slowly.**
ká-lu-náa wâo sâa-sâa — ກະລຸນາເວົ້າຊ້າໆ

**Please repeat.**
ká-lu-náa wâo khéun mai — ກະລຸນາເວົ້າຄືນໃໝ່

**Forgive me, I don't understand.**
khǎw thôht, khàwy baw khào jại — ຂໍໂທດຂ້ອຍບໍ່ເຂົ້າໃຈ

**I/We don't understand.**
baw khào jại — ບໍ່ເຂົ້າໃຈ

**Do you understand?**
jâo khào jại baw — ເຈົ້າເຂົ້າໃຈບໍ່

**What?**
nyǎng — ຫຍັງ

**What did you say?**
jâo wâo nyǎng — ເຈົ້າເວົ້າຫຍັງ

**Can you teach me Lao?**
jâo sǎwn pháa-sǎa láo hâi khàwy dâi baw — ເຈົ້າສອນພາສາ ລາວໃຫ້ຂ້ອຍໄດ້ບໍ່

**What do you call this in Lao?**
ạn-nîi pháa-sǎa láo waa nyǎng — ອັນນີ້ພາສາລາວວ່າຫຍັງ

## nationalities

ສັນຊາດ

| | | |
|---|---|---|
| Where do you come from? | jâo máa tae sai | ເຈົ້າມາແຕ່ໃສ |
| I come from ... | khàwy máa tae ... | ຂ້ອຍມາແຕ່ ... |
| I'm from ... | khàwy pẹn khón ... | ຂ້ອຍເປັນຄົນ ... |
| Australia | ạw-sá-tạa-líi | ອົສຕາລີ |
| Canada | kạa-náa-dạa | ການາດາ |
| China | jịin | ຈີນ |
| Denmark | dạen-mâak | ແດນມາກ |
| England | ạng-kít | ອັງກິດ |
| Europe | yúu-lôhp | ຢູໂລບ |
| France | fa-lang | ຝະລັງ |
| Germany | yóe-la-mán | ເຢຍລະມັນ |
| Holland | háwn-láen | ຮອລແລນ |
| India | in-dia | ອິນເດຍ |
| Italy | íi-tạa-líi | ອີຕາລີ |
| Japan | nyii-pun | ຍີ່ປຸ່ນ |
| Laos | láo | ລາວ |
| New Zealand | níu síi-láen | ນິວຊີແລນ |

**wit & wisdom**

**You don't need to teach an alligator how to swim.**

yaa sạwn khàe láwy nâm ຢ່າສອນແຂ້ລອຍນ້ຳ

SOCIAL

| | | |
|---|---|---|
| **Singapore** | sǐng-a-pọh | ສິງກາໂປ |
| **Spain** | sá-pẹhn | ສະແປນ |
| **Sweden** | sá-wíi-dẹn | ສະວີດເດັນ |
| **Switzerland** | sá-wit-sóe-láen | ສະວິດເຊີແລນ |
| **Taiwan** | tâi-wǎn | ໄຕ້ຫວັນ |
| **USA** | ạa-méh-li-kạa | ອາເມລິກາ |

## age

ອາຍຸ

Asking someone's age is a common question in Laos. It's not considered rude to ask strangers their age.

| | | |
|---|---|---|
| **How old are you?** | jâo ạa-nyu ják pị̣i | ເຈົ້າອາຍຸຈັກປີ |
| **I'm ... years old.** | khàwy ạa-nyu ... pị̣i | ຂ້ອຍອາຍຸ ... ປີ |
| **Very young!** | num lǎai | ໜຸ່ມຫລາຍ |
| **Very old!** | tháo lǎai | ເຖົ້າຫລາຍ |

## occupations

ອາຊີບ

| | | |
|---|---|---|
| **I'm a/an ...** | khàwy pẹn ... | ຂ້ອຍເປັນ ... |
| **artist** | sǐ-la-pịn | ສິລະປິນ |
| **businessperson** | nak thu-la-kít | ນັກທຸລະກິດ |
| **diplomat** | nak kạan-thûut | ນັກການທູດ |
| **doctor** | thaan mǎw | ທ່ານໝໍ |
| **engineer** | wit-sáa-wa-kạwn | ວິຊາວະກອນ |
| **farmer** | sáo-náa | ຊາວນາ |
| **journalist** | nak khao | ນັກຂ່າວ |
| **lawyer** | tha-nái-khwáam | ທະນາຍຄວາມ |
| **musician** | nak dọn-tị̣i | ນັກດົນຕີ |
| **policeman** | tạm lùat | ຕຳຫລວດ |
| **secretary** | léh-khǎa-nu-kạan | ເລຂານຸການ |
| **student** | nak séuk-sǎa | ນັກສຶກສາ |
| **teacher** | khúu | ຄູ |
| **traveller/tourist** | nak thawng thiaw | ນັກທ່ອງທ່ຽວ |

| | | |
|---|---|---|
| volunteer worker | ạa-sǎa-sá-mak kạm-ma-kạwn | ອາສາສະມັກ ກຳມະກອນ |
| I'm in the military. | tha-hǎan | ທະຫານ |
| I'm unemployed. | waang ngáan | ຫວ່າງງານ |

## family

ຄອບຄົວ

Laos is a very family-orientated society, so enquiries about one's family are quite common. If you're asked about marriage or children, it's better to respond with the Lao for 'not yet' rather than 'I/We don't want children' or 'I/We have no plans to get married'.

Lao has no specific word for 'cousin'; if you must refer to this relationship, preface the appropriate Lao word for aunt or uncle with lûuk khǎwng ... (ລູກຂອງ ..., 'child of ...').

**How many in your family?**
khâwp khúa jǎo míi ják khón — ຄອບຄົວເຈົ້າມີຈັກຄົນ

**I have ... in my family.**
**[for numbers, see page 43]**
míi ... khón — ມີ ... ຄົນ

**Are you married (yet)?**
taeng-ngáan lâew lěu baw — ແຕ່ງງານແລ້ວຫລືບໍ່

**Yes, I'm married.**
taeng-ngáan lâew — ແຕ່ງງານແລ້ວ

**I'm not married yet.**
nyáng baw taeng-ngáan — ຍັງບໍ່ແຕ່ງງານ

**I'm single.**
pẹn sóht — ເປັນໂສດ

**Do you have any children (yet)?**
míi lûuk lâew baw — ມີລູກແລ້ວບໍ່

**I have ... child/children.**
míi lûuk ... khón lâew — ມີລູກ ... ຄົນແລ້ວ

**I don't have children yet.**
nyáng baw míi lûuk — ຍັງບໍ່ມີລູກ

## family members

ສະມາຊິກຄອບຄົວ

| | | |
|---|---|---|
| aunt (older sister of either parent) | pâa | ປ້າ |
| child/children | lûuk | ລູກ |
| daughter | lûuk sǎo | ລູກສາວ |
| family | khâwp khúa | ຄອບຄົວ |
| father | phaw | ພໍ່ |
| father's side | | |
| grandfather | púu | ປູ່ |
| grandmother | yaa | ຍ່າ |
| aunt | ạa | ອາ |
| uncle | ao | ອາວ |
| husband | phǔa | ຜົວ |
| mother | mae | ແມ່ |
| mother's side | | |
| grandfather | phaw thào | ພໍ່ເຖົ້າ |
| grandmother | mae thào | ແມ່ເຖົ້າ |
| aunt | nâa | ນ້າ |
| uncle | nâa bao | ນ້າບ່າວ |
| niece/nephew | lǎan | ຫຼານ |
| older sister | êuay | ເອື້ອຍ |

meeting people

## the power behind the elephant

Lao women have substantial gender parity in the workforce, inheritance, land ownership and so on, often more so than in many Western countries. The bad news is that, although women generally fare well in these areas, their cultural standing is a bit further from parity. An oft-repeated Lao saying reminds us that men form the front legs of the elephant, women the hind legs.

Lao Buddhism commonly holds that women must be reborn as men before they can attain nirvana, though many *dhamma* teachers point out that this presumption isn't supported by the suttas (discourses of the Buddha) or by the commentaries. But nevertheless it is a widespread belief.

While many Lao taboos can be bent a little without creating a huge fuss, the following one cannot. Aboard transport such as trucks, buses or riverboats in Laos, women are expected to ride inside. Any attempt to ride on the roof will be immediately discouraged. When asked why women can't sit on the roof, the usual Lao answer is phít sàat-sá-náa – 'it's against the religion', which is to say it's against Lao custom.

Partially this is old-fashioned chivalry – 'it's too dangerous on the roof' – but mainly it's due to a deep-seated superstition that women's bodies should not intentionally occupy a physical space above a man's for fear of damaging men's spiritual status. Men wearing sacred tattoos or amulets often express the fear that such an arrangement will ruin the protection that these symbols are supposed to convey! The superstition runs to how laundry is hung out to dry. Women's clothing – especially underwear – is not to be hung above men's clothing.

| | | |
|---|---|---|
| older brother | âai | ອ້າຍ |
| parents | phaw-mae | ພໍ່ແມ່ |
| relatives | phii-nâwng | ພີ່ນ້ອງ |
| son | lûuk sáai | ລູກຊາຍ |
| uncle (older brother of either parent) | lúng | ລຸງ |
| wife | mía | ເມຍ |
| younger sister | nâwng săo | ນ້ອງສາວ |
| younger brother | nâwng sáai | ນ້ອງຊາຍ |
| younger sibling | náwng | ນ້ອງ |

## feelings

ການສະແດງຄວາມຮູ້ສຶກ

The Lao are much less apt to express their feelings or emotions to strangers than most Western nationalities. Use discretion – any display or expression of strong emotion means a potential loss of face for both speaker and listener.

| | | |
|---|---|---|
| I feel ... | khàwy hûu-séuk ... | ຂ້ອຍຮູ້ສຶກ |
| angry | jại hâai | ໃຈຮ້າຍ |
| excited | teun tên | ຕື່ນເຕັ້ນ |
| happy | dịi jại | ດີໃຈ |
| lonely | ngăo | ເຫງົາ |
| nervous (anxious) | ká-wón ká-wáai | ກະວົນກະວາຍ |
| proud | phúum jại | ພູມໃຈ |
| sad | sâo sòhk | ເສົ້າໂສກ |
| satisfied | pháw jại | ພໍໃຈ |
| sleepy | nguang náwn | ງ້ວງນອນ |
| surprised | pá-láat jại | ປະຫລາດໃຈ |
| tired | meuay | ເໝື່ອຍ |
| upset | ạa-lóm sía | ອາລົມເສຍ |
| I'm bored. | beua | ເບື່ອ |
| This is fun! | muan dịi | ມ່ວນດີ |

meeting people

## opinions

ການອອກຄຳເຫັນ

| | | |
|---|---|---|
| I feel that ... | khàwy hûu-séuk waa ... | ຂ້ອຍຮູ້ສຶກວ່າ ... |
| I think that ... | khàwy khit waa ... | ຂ້ອຍຄິດວ່າ ... |
| I agree. | khàwy hĕn dįi | ຂ້ອຍເຫັນດີ |
| I disagree. | baw hĕn dįi | ບໍ່ເຫັນດີ |
| In my opinion ... | khwáam khit khăwng khàwy ... | ຄວາມຄິດຂອງ ຂ້ອຍ ... |
| As for me ... | săm-láp khàwy ... | ສຳລັບຂ້ອຍ ... |
| It's not important. | baw săm-khán | ບໍ່ສຳຄັນ |

## common interests

ຄວາມສົນໃຈທົ່ວໄປ

**What do you do in your spare time?**
nái wéh-láah wàang jâo het nyăng — ໃນເວລາຫວ້າງ ເຈົ້າເຮັດຫຍັງ

### did you know?

Ká-tâw (ກະຕໍ້), a contest in which a woven rattan – or sometimes plastic – ball approximately 12cm in diameter is kicked around, is almost as popular in Laos as it is in Thailand and Malaysia.

The traditional way to play ká-tâw is for players to stand in a circle (the size of the circle depends on the number of players) and simply try to keep the ball airborne by kicking it soccer-style. Points are scored for style, difficulty and variety of kicking manoeuvres.

A popular variation on ká-tâw – and the one used in local or international competitions – is played with a volleyball net, using all the same rules as in volleyball except that only the feet and head are permitted to touch the ball. It's amazing to see the players perform aerial pirouettes, spiking the ball over the net with their feet.

| | | |
|---|---|---|
| I like ... | khàwy mak ... | ຂ້ອຍມັກ ... |
| I don't like ... | khàwy baw mak ... | ຂ້ອຍບໍ່ມັກ ... |
| Do you like ...? | jâo mak ... baw | ເຈົ້າມັກ ... ບໍ່ |
| art | sí-la-pá | ສິລະປະ |
| cooking | taeng kịn | ແຕ່ງກິນ |
| dancing | fâwn | ຟ້ອນ |
| film | năng leuang | ໜັງເລື່ອງ |
| going out | àwk pại tháang nâwk | ອອກໄປທາງນອກ |
| music | dọn-tịi | ດົນຕີ |
| photography | thaai hûup | ຖ່າຍຮູບ |
| playing games | lìn kẹhm | ຫລິ້ນເກມ |
| playing soccer | lìn bạan-té | ຫລິ້ນບານເຕະ |
| playing sport | lìn kí-láa | ຫລິ້ນກິລາ |
| reading books | aan pêum | ອ່ານປຶ້ມ |
| shopping | pại sêu kheuang | ໄປຊື້ເຄື່ອງ |
| the theatre | boeng la-kháwn | ເບິ່ງລະຄອນ |
| travelling | thawng thiaw | ທ່ອງທ່ຽວ |
| watching TV | boeng thóh-la-that | ເບິ່ງໂທລະທັດ |
| writing | khĭan | ຂຽນ |

## sport

ກິລາ

**Do you like sport?**
jâo mak lìn kí-láa baw — ເຈົ້າມັກຫລິ້ນກິລາບໍ່

**I like playing sport.**
mak lìn kí-láa — ມັກຫລິ້ນກິລາ

**I prefer to watch rather than play sport.**
mak boeng lăai kwaa lìn — ມັກເບິ່ງຫລາຍກ່ວາຫລິ້ນ

**Do you play ...?**
jâo lìn baw ... — ເຈົ້າຫລິ້ນບໍ່ ...

**Would you like to play ...?**
jâo yàak lìn ... baw — ເຈົ້າຢາກຫລິ້ນ ... ບໍ່

| | | |
|---|---|---|
| baseball | bẹhs-bạwn | ເບສບອນ |
| basketball | bạan bâwng | ບານບ້ວງ |
| boxing | tịi múay | ຕີມວຍ |

| | | |
|---|---|---|
| diving | dạm nám | ດຳນ້ຳ |
| gymnastics | kịm-náa-sa-tík | ກິມນາສຕິກ |
| hockey | tịi-khíi thóeng nâm kâwn | ຕີຄີເທິງນ້ຳກ້ອນ |
| keeping fit | hak-săa sú-khá-phâap | ຮັກສາສຸຂະພາບ |
| martial arts | kạan sok múay | ການຊົກມວຍ |
| rugby | lak-bịi | ລັກບີ |
| skiing | lìn sá-kịi | ຫລິ້ນສະກີ |
| soccer (football) | bạan-té | ບານເຕະ |
| swimming | láwy nâm | ລອຍນ້ຳ |
| takraw | ká-tâw | ກະຕໍ່ |
| tennis | tẹn-nîit | ເທັນນິສ |

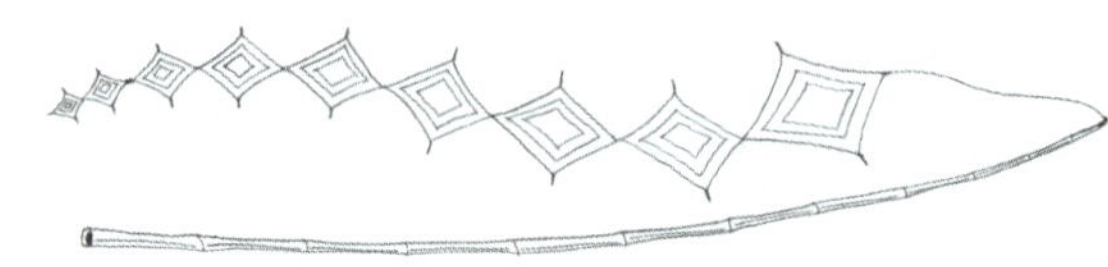

SOCIAL

## weather

ອາກາດ

How's the weather?
ąa-káat pęn jang-dąi — ອາກາດເປັນຈັ່ງໃດ

The weather is nice today.
mêu-nîi ąa-kàat dįi — ມື້ນີ້ອາກາດດີ

The weather isn't good.
ąa-kàat baw dįi — ອາກາດບໍ່ດີ

Is it going to rain?
fŏn sii tók lĕu baw — ຝົນຊິຕົກຫລືບໍ່

It's ...

| | | |
|---|---|---|
| windy | lóm phat | ລົມພັດ |
| not windy | lóm baw phat | ລົມບໍ່ພັດ |
| very cold | năo lăai | ໜາວຫລາຍ |
| very hot | hâwn lăai | ຮ້ອນຫລາຍ |
| raining hard | fŏn tók nak | ຝົນຕົກໜັກ |
| flooding | nám thûam | ນ້ຳຖ້ວມ |

| | | |
|---|---|---|
| cool weather | ąa-kàat yęn | ອາກາດເຢັນ |
| hot weather | ąa-kàat hâwn | ອາກາດຮ້ອນ |
| fog | nâm màwk | ນ້ຳໝອກ |
| lightning | fâa mâep | ຟ້າແມບ |
| monsoon | máw-la-sŭm | ມໍລະສຸມ |
| weather | ąa-kàat | ອາກາດ |

## trekking

ການເດີນປ່າ

Are there guided treks?
mîi pha-nak-ngáan nám thiaw baw dǫen paa — ມີພະນັກງານນຳທ່ຽວບໍ່ເດີນປ່າ

**Do we need a guide?**
jạm pẹn tâwng míi pha-nak-ngáan nám thiaw baw
ຈຳເປັນຕ້ອງມີ ພະນັກງານ ນຳທ່ຽວບໍ່

| | | |
|---|---|---|
| **Does the price include ...?** | láa-kháa huam nám khaa ... baw | ລາຄາຮ່ວມ ນຳຄ່າ ... ບໍ່ |
| **food** | ạa-hăan | ອາຫານ |
| **transport** | khŏn-song | ຂົນສົງ |

**How many hours per day will we walk?**
já nyaang mêu-la ják sua-móhng
ຈະຍ່າງມື້ລະຈັກ ຊົ່ວໂມງ

**Is it a difficult walk?**
tháang pại nyâak baw
ທາງໄປຍາກບໍ່

**I/We would like to hire a guide.**
yàak jâang pha-nak-ngáan nám thiaw
ຢາກຈ້າງ ພະນັກງານນຳທ່ຽວ

| | | |
|---|---|---|
| **backpack** | bạa-lóh/thŏng pêh | ບາໂລ/ຖົງເປ້ |
| **compass** | khĕm thit | ເຂັມທິດ |
| **first-aid kit** | thŏng yáa pá-jạam bạan | ຖົງຢາປະຈັນບ້ານ |
| **guide (person)** | pha-nak-ngáan nám thiaw | ພະນັກງານ ນຳທ່ຽວ |
| **guided trek** | pha-nak ngáan nám thiaw dọen paa | ພະນັກງານນຳ ທ່ຽວເດີນປ່າ |
| **hiking boots** | kòep dọen paa | ເກີບເດີນປ່າ |
| **map** | phăen-thii | ແຜນທີ |
| **mountain climbing** | kạan pịin phúu | ການປີນພູ |
| **provisions** | kheuang dọen paa | ເຄື່ອງເດີນປ່າ |
| **rope** | sêuak | ເຊືອກ |
| **signpost** | pâai bàwk tháang | ປ້າຍບອກທາງ |
| **tour/trek** | thawng thiaw; dọen paa | ທ່ອງທ່ຽວ/ເດີນປ່າ |
| **to walk** | nyaang | ຍ່າງ |

**Where is the trail to ...?**
tháang pại ... yuu săi
ທາງໄປ ... ຢູ່ໃສ

**Which is the shortest route?**
tháang dại sàn kwaa
ທາງໃດສັ້ນກວ່າ

**Which is the easiest route?**
tháang dại sá-dùak kwaa
ທາງໃດສະດວກກ່ວາ

**Where's the nearest village?**

muu bâan thii yuu kâi kwaa muu săi | ໝູ່ບ້ານທີ່ຢູ່ໃກ້ ກ່ວາໝູ່ຢູ່ໃສ

**Is it safe to climb this mountain?**

khêun phuu nîi pàwt pháí baw | ຂຶ້ນພູນີ້ປອດໄພບໍ່

**Is there a hut up there?**

yuu thóeng phúu míi thĭang hai baw | ຢູ່ເທິງພູມີຖຽງໄຮ່ບໍ່

**I'd like to talk to someone who knows this area.**

yàak lóm káp phûu hûu phêun thii nîi | ຢາກລົມກັບຜູ້ຮູ້ພື້ນທີ່ນີ້

**How far is it from ... to ...?**

tae ... thŏeng ... kại thao dại | ແຕ່ ... ເຖິງ ... ໄກເທົ່າໃດ

**Where have you come from?**

jâo máa tae săi | ເຈົ້າມາແຕ່ໃສ

**How long did it take you?**

jâo sâi wéh-láa lăai pạan dại | ເຈົ້າໃຊ້ເວລາຫລາຍ ປານໃດ

| **How many ...?** | ják ... | ຈັກ ... |
|---|---|---|
| **days** | mêu | ມື້ |
| **hours** | sua-móhng | ຊົວໂມງ |
| **kilometres** | kí-lóh-maet | ກິໂລແມັດ |
| **metres** | maet | ແມັດ |

**I'm lost.**

khàwy lŏng tháang | ຂ້ອຍຫລົງທາງ

**Does this path go to ...?**

tháang nîi pại hâwt ... | ທາງນີ້ໄປຮອດ ...

**How long is the trail?**

tháang nyáo pạan dại | ທາງຍາວປານໃດ

**Is the track well-marked?**

míi pâai bàwk tháang baw | ມີປ້າຍບອກທາງບໍ່

**Can we go through here?**

phaan tháang nîi dâi baw | ຜ່ານທາງນີ້ໄດ້ບໍ່

**When does it get dark?**

ják móhng sii mêut | ຈັກໂມງຊິມືດ

**Where can we buy supplies?**

sêu kheuang sâi dâi yuu săi | ຊື້ເຄື່ອງໃຊ້ໄດ້ຢູ່ໃສ

**Who lives here?**
phăi yuu bawn nîi — ໃຜຢູ່ບ່ອນນີ້

**Can I/we stay in this village?**
khàwy/phŭak háo phak yuu bâan nîi dâi baw — ຂ້ອຍ/ພວກເຮົາພັກຢູ່ບ້ານນີ້ໄດ້ບໍ່

**Can I/we sleep here?**
khàwy/phŭak háo náwn yuu nîi dâi baw — ຂ້ອຍ/ພວກເຮົານອນຢູ່ນີ້ໄດ້ບໍ່

| | | |
|---|---|---|
| **blanket** | phàa hom | ຜ້າຫົ່ມ |
| **hill tribe (High Lao)** | sáo khăo | ຊາວເຂົາ |
| **lodging** | bawn phak | ບ່ອນພັກ |
| **medicine** | yąa | ຢາ |
| **mosquito coil** | yąa jút kąn nyúng | ຢາຈຸດກັນຍຸງ |
| **mosquitoes** | nyúng | ຍຸງ |
| **mosquito net** | mûng | ມຸ້ງ |
| **opium** | yąa fin | ຢາຝິ່ນ |
| **raft** | pháe | ແພ |
| **village headman** | nai bâan | ນາຍບ້ານ |
| **water** | nâm | ນ້ຳ |

## camping

ການຕັ້ງຄ່າຍ

In general, the Lao government permits foreigners to camp outdoors only when they are participating in a tour led by a Lao PDR-licensed tour agency. This may change as Laos opens further to tourism.

| | | |
|---|---|---|
| **camping** | kąan tâng khêm | ການຕັ້ງເຄັ້ມ |
| **campsite** | bawn tâng khêm | ບ່ອນຕັ້ງເຄັ້ມ |
| **rope** | sêuak | ເຊືອກ |
| **sleeping bag** | thŏng náwn | ຖົງນອນ |
| **tent** | tùup phàa | ຕູບຜ້າ |
| **torch (flashlight)** | fái săai | ໄຟສາຍ |

**Is there a campsite nearby?**
yuu kâi nîi míi bawn tâng khêm baw — ຢູ່ໃກ້ນີ້ມີບ່ອນຕັ້ງເຄັ້ມບໍ່

**Where's the nearest campsite?**
bawn tâng khêm thii kâi thii sút yuu săi — ບ່ອນຕັ້ງເຄັ້ມທີ່ໃກ້ທີ່ສຸດຢູ່ໃສ

**Is drinking water available?**
míi nâm deum baw — ມີນ້ຳດື່ມບໍ່

**Can I/we put a tent here?**
[khàwy; phûak háo] táng tùup phàa yuu nîi dâi baw — ຂ້ອຍ; ພວກເຮົາ ຕັ້ງຕູບຜ້າຢູ່ນີ້ໄດ້ບໍ່

**Is it safe?**
pàwt phái baw — ປອດໄພບໍ່

## cycling

ການຂີ່ລົດຖີບ

Bicycles are a popular form of transport throughout urban Laos and can be hired cheaply almost anywhere there are guesthouses. These Thai- or Chinese-made street bikes come in varying degrees of usability, so be sure to inspect the bikes thoroughly before renting. Lao customs doesn't object to visitors bringing bicycles into the country.

**Where can I hire a bike?**
khàwy já sao lot thìip dâi yuu săi — ຂ້ອຍຈະເຊົ່າລົດຖີບໄດ້ຢູ່ໃສ

| | | |
|---|---|---|
| **How much is it for ...?** | khaa sao thao dąai taw ... | ຄ່າເຊົ່າເທົ່າໃດຕໍ່ ... |
| **an hour** | neung sua-móhng | ໜຶ່ງຊົ່ວໂມງ |
| **the morning** | tąwn sâo | ຕອນເຊົ້າ |
| **the afternoon** | tąwn baai | ຕອນບ່າຍ |
| **the day** | neung wan | ໜຶ່ງວັນ |

**Where can I find second-hand bikes for sale?**
mĭi lot thìip méu sǎwng khǎai yuu sǎi — ມີລົດຖີບມືສອງຂາຍຢູ່ໃສ

**Is it within cycling distance?**
tháang nîi pęn wóng jąwn sǎm-láp khii lot thìip baw — ທາງນີ້ເປັນວົງຈອນສຳລັບຂີ່ລົດຖີບບໍ່

**Is the trail suitable for bikes?**
tháang nîi máw sǎm-láp khii lot thìip baw — ທາງນີ້ເໝາະສຳລັບຂີ່ລົດຖີບບໍ່

**I have a flat tyre.**
tįin lot khàwy hua — ຕີນລົດຂ້ອຍຮົ່ວ

| | | |
|---|---|---|
| **bicycle** | lot thìip | ລົດຖີບ |
| **brakes** | hàam | ຫ້າມ |
| **to cycle** | thìip | ຖີບ |
| **gear stick** | khan kįa | ຄັນເກຍ |
| **handlebars** | khǎo | ເຂົາ |
| **helmet** | mùak kąn nawk | ໝວກກັນນ໊ອກ |
| **inner tube** | yáang nái | ຢາງໃນ |
| **lights** | fái tąa | ໄຟຕາ |
| **padlock** | ká-jąe | ກະແຈ |
| **pump** | kâwng sùup | ກ້ອງສູບ |
| **puncture** | hua | ຮົ່ວ |
| **saddle** | ąan | ອານ |
| **wheel** | kǫng lot | ກົງລົດ |

## geography

ພູມີສາດ

Many town and village names in Laos incorporate the following geographic or demographic features.

| | | |
|---|---|---|
| Ban or Baan (village) | bâan | ບ້ານ |
| Don (river island) | dạwn | ດອນ |
| Khok or Kok (knoll or mound) | khôhk | ໂຄກ |
| Muang (city or district) | méuang | ເມືອງ |
| Nakhon (large city) | na-kháwn | ນະຄອນ |
| Nam (river in Northern Laos) | nâm | ນ້ຳ |
| Non (hill, knoll or mound) | nóhn | ໂນນ |
| Nong (pond/lake) | nǎwng | ໜອງ |
| Pak (mouth – usually at a river mouth) | pàak | ປາກ |
| Se (rivers in Southern Laos) | séh | ເຊ |
| Vieng (city) | wíang | ວຽງ |
| Xieng (city) | síang | ຊຽງ |

## geographic features

ພູມມີປະເທດອື່ນ

| | | |
|---|---|---|
| cave | thàm | ຖ້ຳ |
| cliff | phǎa | ຜາ |
| countryside | bâan nâwk | ບ້ານນອກ |
| field (dry) | hai | ໄຮ່ |
| footpath | tháang nyaang | ທາງຍ່າງ |
| forest | paa | ປ່າ |
| hill | phúu nâwy | ພູນ້ອຍ |
| jungle | dọng | ດົງ |
| mountain | phúu khǎo | ພູເຂົາ |
| mountain peak | jạwm phúu | ຈອມພູ |

a potted history

## plain of jars

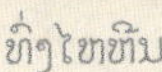

Among the most enigmatic sights in Laos are several meadow-like areas in Xieng Khuang Province littered with large stone jars. Quite a few theories have been advanced as to the functions of the stone jars – that they were used as sarcophagi, as wine fermenters or for rice storage – but the most likely theory suggests they held relics associated with ritual reburial. White quartzite rocks have also been found lying next to some of the jars, along with vases that may have contained human remains.

Aerial photographic evidence suggests that a thin 'track' of jars may link the various jar sites in Xieng Khuang, and some researchers hope future excavations will uncover sealed jars whose contents may be relatively intact.

The jars are commonly said to be 2000 years old, but in the absence of any organic material associated with the jars – eg, bones or food remains – there's no reliable way to date them. The jars may be associated with the equally mysterious stone megaliths found off Route 6 on the way north to Sam Neua, and/or with large Dongson drum-shaped stone objects discovered in Luang Prabang Province. All of the unanswered questions regarding the Plain of Jars (**thong hǎi hǐn**) make this area ripe for archaeological investigation, a proceeding that has been slowed by years of war and by the presence of UXO (unexploded ordnance).

Site 1, 15km south-west of Phonsavan and the largest of the various sites, features 250 jars which weigh from 600kg to one tonne each; the biggest of them weighs as much as six tonnes. The jars have been fashioned from solid stone, most from a tertiary conglomerate known as molasses, akin to sandstone, and a few from granite.

| | | |
|---|---|---|
| rice field (wet) | náa | ນາ |
| river | nâm | ນ້ຳ |
| river rapids | kâeng | ແກ້ງ |
| riverbank | fang nâm | ຝັ່ງນ້ຳ |
| sea | tha-léh | ທະເລ |
| spring/well | baw nâm | ບໍ່ນ້ຳ |
| stone | hĭn | ຫີນ |
| stream | hùay | ຫ້ວຍ |
| swamp | bẹung | ບຶງ |
| trail | tháang thiaw | ທາງທ່ຽວ |
| waterfall | nâm tók tàat | ນ້ຳຕົກຕາດ |

## animals

ສັດປ່າ

| | | |
|---|---|---|
| ant | mót | ໝົດ |
| banteng (type of wild cattle) | ngúa dàeng | ງົວແດງ |
| barking deer | fáan | ຟານ |
| bear | mĭi | ໝີ |
| bee | mae phòeng | ແມ່ເຜີ້ງ |
| bird | nok | ນົກ |
| butterfly | máeng ká-bêua | ແມງກະເບື້ອ |
| civet | ngĭan | ເຫງັນ |
| cockroach | máeng sàap | ແມງສາບ |
| cow | ngúa | ງົວ |

SOCIAL

| | | |
|---|---|---|
| **crocodile** | khàe | ແຂ້ |
| **deer** | kwạang | ກວາງ |
| **dog** | mǎa | ໝາ |
| **dolphin** | pạa lóh-máa | ປາໂລມາ |
| **duck** | pét | ເປັດ |
| **elephant** | sâang | ຊ້າງ |
| **fish** | pạa | ປາ |
| **fishing cat** | sěua pạa | ເສືອປາ |
| **fly** | máeng wán | ແມງວັນ |
| **frog** | kóp | ກົບ |
| **gaur** | ká-thíng | ກະທິງ |
| **gecko** | káp-kâe | ກັບແກ້ |
| **gibbon** | sa-níi | ຊະນີ |
| **horse** | mâa | ມ້າ |
| **leaf monkey** | khaang | ຄ່າງ |
| **leopard** | sěua dạo | ເສືອດາວ |
| **monkey** | líng | ລິງ |
| **rabbit** | ká-tại | ກະຕ່າຍ |
| **rhinoceros** | hâet | ແຮດ |
| **scorpion** | máeng ngáo | ແມງເງົາ |
| **shrimp** | kûng | ກຸ້ງ |
| **snake** | ngúu | ງູ |
| **snake (venomous)** | ngúu phít | ງູພິດ |
| **tiger** | sěua khong | ເສືອໂຄ່ງ |
| **turtle** | tao | ເຕົ່າ |
| **water buffalo** | khu-wáai | ຄວາຍ |
| **water fowl** | nok nâm | ນົກນ້ຳ |
| **wild animals** | sát paa | ສັດປ່າ |
| **wild buffalo** | khuáai paa | ຄວາຍປ່າ |
| **young animal; offspring** | lûuk sát | ລູກສັດ |

## did you know?

The *dipterocarp* is a member of a family of evergreen trees commonly found in south Asia and Africa, named for its helicopter-like seed pods. It's generally a large tree, known for its leathery leaves and aromatic resins. The tree can be used as a source of timber and in the production of varnishes and herbal remedies.

# plants

ພືດ

| | | |
|---|---|---|
| **bamboo** | phai | ໄຜ່ |
| **dipterocarp** | yáang | ຍາງ |
| **flower** | dàwk mâi | ດອກໄມ້ |
| **grass/herb** | nyàa | ຫຍ້າ |
| **pine** | tôn sŏn | ຕົ້ນສົນ |
| **tree** | tôn mâi | ຕົ້ນໄມ້ |
| **teak** | tôn sák | ຕົ້ນສັກ |

# FOOD

## ອາຫານ

Lao cuisine is similar to Thai cuisine in many ways. Almost all dishes are cooked using fresh ingredients, including vegetables, fish, poultry, pork and beef or water buffalo.

Except for one-dish rice plates and noodle dishes, Lao meals are usually ordered family style, which is to say that two or more people order together, sharing different dishes. Traditionally, the party orders one of each kind of dish, eg, one salad, one stir-fry, one soup, etc. Each dish is generally large enough for two people. Extras may be ordered for a large party.

Because of Laos' distance from the sea, freshwater fish is more commonly used than saltwater fish or shellfish. To salt the food, various fermented fish concoctions are used, most commonly nâm pąa (ນ້ຳປາ), which is a thin sauce of fermented anchovies (usually imported from Thailand), and pąa dàek (ປາແດກ), a coarser, native Lao preparation that includes chunks of fermented freshwater fish, rice husks and rice 'dust'. Nâm pąa dàek (ນ້ຳປາແດກ) is the sauce poured from pąa dàek.

Many Lao dishes are quite spicy because of the Lao penchant for chillies or màak phét (ໝາກເຜັດ). But the Lao also eat a lot of what could be called Chinese food which is generally, but not always, less spicy.

Rice is the foundation for all Lao meals (as opposed to snacks), as elsewhere in South-East Asia. In general, the Lao eat 'sticky' or glutinous rice (ເຂົ້າໜຽວ, khào nĭaw), although ordinary steamed white rice (ເຂົ້າໜຶ້ງ, khào nèung) is also common. Sticky rice is served in lidded baskets and eaten with the hands: the general practice is to grab a small fistful from the woven container that sits on the table, then roll it into a rough ball which is used to dip into the various dishes. Khào nèung, on the other hand, is eaten with a fork and spoon. The fork is only used to prod food onto the spoon, which is the main utensil for eating this type of rice. Chopsticks (ໄມ້ທູ່, mâi thuu) are only used for eating fŏe (ເຝີ) or other Chinese noodle dishes.

## at the restaurant

ຢູ່ຮ້ານອາຫານ

| | | |
|---|---|---|
| Please bring (a) ... | khǎw ... dae | ຂໍ ... ແດ່ |
| bill | saek | ແຊັກ |
| bowl | thùay | ຖ້ວຍ |
| chopsticks | mâi thuu | ໄມ້ທູ່ |
| fork | sâwm | ສ້ອມ |
| glass | jàwk | ຈອກ |
| knife | mîit | ມີດ |
| menu | láai-kạan ạa-hǎan | ລາຍການອາຫານ |
| plate | jạan | ຈານ |
| spoon | buang | ບ່ວງ |

I don't like it hot and spicy.
baw mak phét — ບໍ່ມັກເຜັດ

I like it hot and spicy.
mak phét — ມັກເຜັດ

I can eat Lao food.
kịn ạa-hǎan láo dâi — ກິນອາຫານລາວໄດ້

Do you have ...?
míi ... baw — ມີ ... ບໍ່

What do you have that's special?
míi nyǎng phi-sèt baw — ມີຫຍັງພິເສດບໍ່

I'd like to try that.
khàwy yàak láwng kịn boeng — ຂ້ອຍຢາກລອງກິນເບິ່ງ

I didn't order this.
khàwy baw dâi sang náew nîi — ຂ້ອຍບໍ່ໄດ້ສັ່ງແນວນີ້

delicious
sâep — ແຊບ

### wit & wisdom

It's easy to earn money but difficult to find kindness.

ngóen khám hǎa dâi, — ເງິນຄຳຫາໄດ້
nâm jại hǎa yàak — ນ້ຳໃຈຫາຍາກ

## vegetarian meals

ອາຫານເຈ

Those visitors who wish to avoid eating animal food while in Laos can be accommodated only with extreme effort. Chinese restaurants are your best bet since many Chinese Buddhists eat vegetarian food during Buddhist festivals. More often than not, however, visiting vegetarians are left to their own devices at the average restaurant.

**I eat only vegetables.**
khàwy kịn tae phák — ຂ້ອຍກິນແຕ່ຜັກ

**I can't eat pork.**
khàwy kịn mŭu baw dâi — ຂ້ອຍກິນຊີ້ນໝູບໍ່ໄດ້

**I can't eat beef.**
khàwy kịn sìin ngúa baw dâi — ຂ້ອຍກິນງົວບໍ່ໄດ້

**I don't want any meat.**
khàwy baw ạo sìin sát — ຂ້ອຍບໍ່ເອົາຊີ້ນສັດ

**No fish or chicken.**
baw sai pạa lĕu kai — ບໍ່ໃສ່ປາຫລືໄກ່

**I/We want vegetables only.**
**(see Vegetables, page 145)**
ạo phák thao nân — ເອົາຜັກເທົ່ານັ້ນ

**Please don't use fish sauce.**
ká-lu-náa baw sai nâm pạa — ກະລຸນາບໍ່ໃສ່ນ້ຳປາ

**Please don't use padaek.**
ká-lu-náa baw sai pạa dàek — ກະລຸນາບໍ່ໃສ່ປາແດກ

**Please don't use MSG.**
ká-lu-náa baw sai pâeng núa — ກະລຸນາບໍ່ໃສ່ແປ້ງນົວ

| | | |
|---|---|---|
| soy sauce | nâm sá-ìu | ນ້ຳສະອີ້ວ |
| tofu (soybean curd) | tâo-hûu | ເຕົາຮູ້ |
| vegetable oil | nâm-mán phêut | ນ້ຳມັນພືດ |

## staples

ອາຫານຫຼັກ

| | | |
|---|---|---|
| beef | sìin ngúa | ຊີ້ນງົວ |
| chicken | kai | ໄກ່ |
| fish | pąa | ປາ |
| pork | sìin mŭu | ຊີ້ນໝູ |
| rice | khào | ເຂົ້າ |
| seafood | ąa-hăan tha-léh | ອາຫານທະເລ |
| shrimp/prawns | kûng | ກຸ້ງ |
| vegetables | phak | ຜັກ |
| water buffalo | sìin khuáai | ຊີ້ນຄວາຍ |

## rice dishes

ອາຫານກັບເຂົ້າ

| | | |
|---|---|---|
| steamed white rice | khào nèung | ເຂົ້າໜຶ້ງ |
| sticky rice | khào nĭaw | ເຂົ້າໜຽວ |
| curry over rice | khào làat kąeng | ເຂົ້າລາດແກງ |
| 'red' pork (char siu) with rice | khào mŭu dąeng | ເຂົ້າໝູແດງ |
| roast duck over rice | khào nàa pét | ເຂົ້າໜ້າເປັດ |
| fried rice with ... | khào phát (khào khùa) ... | ເຂົ້າຜັດ (ເຂົ້າຂົ້ວ) ... |
| chicken | kai | ໄກ່ |
| pork | mŭu | ໝູ |
| shrimp/prawns | kûng | ກຸ້ງ |
| crab | pųu | ປູ |

FOOD

# noodles

ເຝີ/ໝີ່

Fŏe (ເຝີ), perhaps the most common food sold anywhere in Laos, are flat noodles made with rice flour. Heavier wheat noodles – sometimes made with egg, sometimes not – are known as mii (ໝີ່). You'll find both kinds noodles in most Lao restaurants and in small hàan fŏe (noodle shops). Slivers of beef or pork are the usual accompaniments, though occasionally chicken may be available. Because of their Chinese origins, noodles are usually eaten with chopsticks (and a spoon if served in a broth).

Fŏe is quite popular as a snack or even for breakfast, and is almost always served with a plate of fresh lettuce, mint, coriander, mung-bean sprouts, lime wedges and sometimes basil, for adding to the soup as desired. In some places – especially in the south – people mix their own fŏe sauce of lime, crushed fresh chilli, fermented shrimp paste (ກະປິ, ká-pí) and sugar at the table using a little saucer provided for that purpose.

fŏe ເຝີ
**rice noodle soup with vegetables and meat**

fŏe hàeng ເຝີແຫ້ງ
**rice noodles with vegetables and meat, no broth**

làat nàa ລາດໜ້າ
**rice noodles with gravy**

fŏe khùa ເຝີຂົ້ວ
**fried rice noodles with meat and vegetables**

phát sá-ìu ຜັດສະອິ້ວ
**fried rice noodles with soy sauce**

mii nâm ໝີ່ນ້ຳ
**yellow wheat noodles in broth, with vegetables and meat**

mii hàeng ໝີ່ແຫ້ງ
**yellow wheat noodles with vegetables and meat**

khào pûn ເຂົ້າປຸ້ນ
**white flour noodles served with sweet-spicy sauce**

## bread & pastries

ເຂົ້າຈີ່ແລະເຂົ້າໜົມ

plain bread (usually French-style)
khào jii — ເຂົ້າຈີ່

baguette sandwich
khào jii páa-tê — ເຂົ້າຈີ່ປາເຕ

croissants
khúa-sawng — ຄົວຊ່ອງ

'Chinese doughnuts' (Mandarin youtiao)
pá-thawng-kó (khào-nǒm khuu) — ປະຖ່ອງໂກະ(ເຂົ້າໜົມຄູ່)

## eggs

ໄຂ່

| | | |
|---|---|---|
| egg | khai | ໄຂ່ |
| fried egg | khai dạo | ໄຂ່ດາວ |
| hard-boiled egg | khai tôm | ໄຂ່ຕົ້ມ |
| plain omelette | jẹun khai | ຈືນໄຂ່ |
| scrambled egg | khai khùa | ໄຂ່ຂົ້ວ |

## appetisers ('drinking food')

ກັບແກ້ມ

Káp kâem (ກັບແກ້ມ) are dishes intended to be eaten on picnics or while drinking beer, lào láo (ເຫຼົ້າລາວ, rice alcohol) or other alcoholic beverages. English-language menus in Laos may translate such dishes as 'snacks' or 'appetisers'. You can also order káp kâem with regular meals, although they will usually be served before other kinds of dishes.

| | | |
|---|---|---|
| **cellophane noodle salad** | yám sèn wûn | ຍຳເສັ້ນຫວຸ້ນ |
| **dried water buffalo skin** | nǎng khuáai hàeng | ໜັງຄວາຍແຫ້ງ |
| **fried peanuts** | thua dịn jẹun | ຖົ່ວດິນຈືນ |
| **fried potatoes** | mán fa-lang jẹun | ມັນຝລັງຈືນ |
| **fresh spring rolls** | yáw díp | ຍໍດິບ |
| **fried spring rolls** | yáw jẹun | ຍໍຈືນ |
| **shrimp chips** | khào khìap kûng | ເຂົ້າຂຽບກຸ້ງ |
| **spicy green papaya salad** | tạm màak-hung | ຕຳໝາກຫຸງ |
| **spicy grilled chicken** | pîng kai | ປີ້ງໄກ່ |
| **toasted pork** | pîng mǔu | ປີ້ງໝູ |

## meat salads

ລາບ

One of the most common Lao dishes is làap (ລາບ), which is a salad of minced meat, chicken or fish tossed with lime juice, garlic, khào khùa (ເຂົ້າຂົ້ວ, roast, powdered sticky rice), green onions, mint leaves and chillies. It can be very hot or rather mild, depending on the cook or your own request. Làap is typically served with a large plate of lettuce, mint and steamed mango leaves. Using your fingers, you wrap a little làap in the lettuce and herbs and eat it with hand-rolled balls of sticky rice.

| | | |
|---|---|---|
| **beef laap** | làap sìin | ລາບຊີ້ນ |
| **chicken laap** | làap kai | ລາບໄກ່ |
| **fish laap** | làap pạa | ລາບປາ |
| **pork laap** | làap mǔu | ລາບໝູ |

## soup

ແກງ

| | | |
|---|---|---|
| fish and lemongrass soup with mushrooms | | |
| tôm yám pạa | | ຕົ້ມຍຳປາ |
| mild soup with vegetables and pork | | |
| kạeng jèut | | ແກງຈືດ |
| same as above, with bean curd | | |
| kạeng jèut tâo-hûu | | ແກງຈືດເຕົາຮູ້ |
| rice soup with ... | khào pìak ... | ເຂົ້າປຽກ ... |
| chicken | kai | ໄກ່ |
| fish | pạa | ປາ |
| pork | mǔu | ໝູ |

## stir-fried dishes

ອາຫານປະເພດຂົ້ວ

| | |
|---|---|
| beef in oyster sauce | |
| ngúa phàt nâm-mán hǎwy | ງົວຜັດນ້ຳມັນຫອຍ |
| chicken with ginger | |
| kai phát khǐing | ໄກ່ຜັດຂີງ |
| chicken fried with chillies | |
| kai phát màak phét | ໄກ່ຜັດໝາກເຜັດ |
| chicken with mushrooms | |
| kai phát hét | ໄກ່ຜັດເຫັດ |
| stir-fried mixed vegetables | |
| phát phák | ຜັດຜັກ |
| sweet and sour pork | |
| mǔu sòm-wǎan | ໝູສົ້ມຫວານ |

## fish

ປາ

| | | |
|---|---|---|
| crisp-fried fish | jęun pąa | ຈືນປາ |
| fried prawns | jęun kûng | ຈືນກຸ້ງ |
| grilled prawns | pįing kûng | ປີ້ງກຸ້ງ |
| steamed fish | nèung pąa | ໜຶ້ງປາ |
| grilled fish | pįing pąa | ປີ້ງປາ |
| sweet & sour fish | pąa sòm-wăan | ປາສົ້ມຫວານ |
| catfish | pąa dúk | ປາດຸກ |
| carp | pąa pàak | ປາປ່າກ |
| eel | ian | ອ່ຽນ |
| freshwater stingray | pąa făa lái | ປາຝາໄລ |
| giant Mekong catfish | pąa béuk | ປາບຶກ |
| serpent fish | pąa khaw | ປາຄໍ່ |
| sheatfish | pąa sa-ngûa | ປາສະງົ້ວ |

## vegetables

ຜັກ

| | | |
|---|---|---|
| bamboo shoots | naw mâi | ໜໍ່ໄມ້ |
| bean | thua | ຖົວ |
| bean sprouts | thua ngâwk | ຖົວງອກ |
| bitter melon | máa-láa-jįin (màak ha) | ມາລາຈີນ (ໝາກຮະ) |
| cabbage | ká-lam pįi | ກະລໍ່າປີ |
| cauliflower | ká-lam pįi dàwk | ກະລໍ່າປີດອກ |
| Chinese radish (daikon) | phák kàat hŭa | ຜັກກາດຫົວ |

### wit & wisdom

**When choosing an elephant, check the tail; when choosing a wife, look at her mother.**

lêuak sang hài boeng hăang, — ເລືອກຊ້າງໃຫ້ເບິ່ງຫາງ
lêuak náan hài boeng mae — ເລືອກນາງໃຫ້ເບິ່ງແມ່

food

| | | |
|---|---|---|
| **corn** | khào săa-líi | ເຂົ້າສາລີ |
| **cucumber** | màak tạeng | ໝາກແຕງ |
| **eggplant** | màak khěua | ໝາກເຂືອ |
| **garlic** | hŭa phák thíam | ຫົວຜັກທຽມ |
| **lettuce** | phák sá-lat | ຜັກສະລັດ |
| **long green beans** | thua nyáo | ຖົ່ວຍາວ |
| **lotus root** | tôn bụa | ຕົ້ນບົວ |
| **onion** | hŭa phák bua | ຫົວຜັກບົ່ວ |
| **onion (green 'scallions')** | tôn phák bua | ຕົ້ນຜັກບົ່ວ |
| **peanuts** | màak thua dịn | ໝາກຖົ່ວດິນ |
| **potato** | mán fa-lang | ມັນຝລັ່ງ |
| **pumpkin** | màak éu (màak fák) | ໝາກອຶ (ໝາກຟັກ) |
| **tomato** | màak len | ໝາກເລັ່ນ |

## condiments, herbs & spices

ເຄື່ອງປຸງ, ເຄື່ອງຫອມແລະເຄື່ອງເທດ

Along with chillies, lime juice, lemon grass and fresh coriander leaf are added to give Lao food its characteristic tang. Nâm pạa (ນ້ຳປາ), a thin, clear fish sauce made from fermented anchovies, or ká-pí, fermented shrimp paste, provide the cuisine's main salty element.

Other common seasonings include hot chillies, ground peanuts, tamarind juice, lime juice, ginger and coconut milk. Chillies are sometimes served on the side in hot pepper sauces called jaew (ແຈ່ວ).

Granulated salt and ground black pepper are almost never present on a Lao table, although they may be used during the cooking. Soy sauce can be requested, though this is normally used as a condiment for Chinese food only.

| | | |
|---|---|---|
| **chilli** | màak phét | ໝາກເຜັດ |
| **coconut extract** | nâm ká-thí | ນ້ຳກະທິ |
| **coriander (cilantro)** | phák hăwm | ຜັກຫອມ |
| **dipping sauces** | jaew | ແຈ່ວ |
| **dried shrimp** | kûng hàeng | ກຸ້ງແຫ້ງ |

| | | |
|---|---|---|
| **fish sauce** | nâm pąa | ນ້ຳປາ |
| **fish sauce with chillies** | nâm pąa sai màak phét | ນ້ຳປາໃສ່ໝາກເຜັດ |
| **ginger** | khĭing | ຂີງ |
| **ground peanuts** | thua dįn | ຖົ່ວດິນ |
| **lemongrass** | hŭa sŏng khái | ຫົວສິງໄຄ |
| **lime juice** | nâm màak náo | ນ້ຳໝາກນາວ |
| **salt** | kęua | ເກືອ |
| **sesame** | màak ngáa | ໝາກງາ |
| **soy sauce** | nâm sá-ĭu | ນ້ຳສະອີ໊ວ |
| **sugar** | nâm-tąan | ນ້ຳຕານ |
| **sweet basil** | bąi hŏh-la-pháa | ໃບໂຫລະພາ |
| **tamarind** | màak khăam | ໝາກຂາມ |
| **vinegar** | nâm sòm | ນ້ຳສົ້ມ |

## cooking methods

ວິທີປຸງແຕ່ງອາຫານ

| | |
|---|---|
| óp<br>**baked** | ອົບ |
| tôm<br>**boiled** | ຕົ້ມ |
| súk<br>**cooked/ripe** | ສຸກ |
| kąeng<br>**curried** | ແກງ |
| jęun<br>**fried in large pieces** | ຈືນ |
| khùa phák thíam phik thái<br>**fried with garlic and black pepper** | ຂົ້ວຜັກທຽມພິກໄທ |
| khùa khĭing<br>**fried with ginger** | ຂົ້ວຂີງ |
| pîing<br>**grilled, barbecued or roasted** | ປີ້ງ |
| díp<br>**raw/unripe** | ດິບ |
| nèung<br>**steamed (fish, rice only)** | ໜື້ງ |

## tropical delights

Laos, like its South-East Asian neighbours, offers travellers an opportunity to indulge in a wide range of tropical fruit – don't miss out!

ໝາກພ້າວ — màak phâo

**coconut** – grated for cooking when mature, eaten with a spoon when young; juice is sweetest in young coconuts (year-round)

ໝາກຂຽບ — màak khìap

**custard-apple** (July to October)

ທຸລຽນ — thu-lían

**durian** – held in high esteem by South-East Asians, but most Westerners dislike this fruit. There are several varieties and seasons, so keep trying.

ໝາກສີດາ — màak sĭi-dạa

**guava** (year-round)

ໝາກມີ້ — màak mîi

**jackfruit** – similar in outward appearance to durian but much easier to take (year-round)

ໝາກນາວ — màak náo

**lime** (year-round)

ໝາກຍຳໄຍ — màak nyám nyái

**longan** – 'dragon's eyes', small, brown, spherical, similar to rambutan (July to October)

FOOD

ໝາກລິ້ນຈີ່ màak lîn-jii
**lychee** (July to October)

ໝາກມ່ວງ màak muang
**mango** – several varieties and seasons

ໝາກມັງຄຸດ màak máng-khut
**mangosteen** – round, purple fruit with juicy white flesh (April to September)

ໝາກນັດ màak nat
**pineapple** (year-round)

ໝາກຫຸ່ງ màak hung
**papaya** (year-round)

ໝາກເງາະ màak ngaw
**rambutan** – red, hairy-skinned fruit with grape-like interior (July to September)

ໝາກກຽງ màak kįang
**rose-apple** – small, apple-like texture, very fragrant (April to July)

ອ້ອຍ âwy
**sugarcane** (year-round)

ໝາກຂາມ màak khǎam
**tamarind** – comes in sweet as well as tart varieties (year-round)

khùa (phát) — ຂົ້ວ (ຜັດ)
stir-fried or fried in small pieces

## fruit

ໝາກໄມ້

**apple (usually imported, year-round)**
màak pọhm — ໝາກໂປມ
**banana (year-round)**
màak kûay — ໝາກກ້ວຍ
**mandarin orange (year-round)**
màak kîang — ໝາກກ້ຽງ
**watermelon (year-round)**
màak móh — ໝາກໂມ

## sweets

ເຂືອງຫວານ

Restaurant menus rarely offer Lao sweets (ເຂືອງຫວານ, kheuang wǎan). Instead the Lao buy these fresh in local morning markets or from street vendors in the evening. Typical ingredients include sticky rice, rice flour, palm and cane sugar, agar-agar (gelatin made from a type of seaweed), shredded coconut, coconut extract, egg yolks and various kinds of fruit.

**banana in coconut milk**
nâm wǎan màak kûay — ນ້ຳຫວານໝາກກ້ວຍ
**cakes made with sticky rice flour**
khào nǒm — ເຂົ້າໜົມ
**custard**
khào sǎng-kha-nyǎa — ສັງຂະຫຍາ
**egg custard**
khào-nǒm màw kạeng — ເຂົ້າໜົມໝໍ້ແກງ
**red sticky rice in coconut cream**
khào nǐaw dạeng — ເຂົ້າໜຽວແດງ

FOOD

**sticky rice in coconut cream and ripe mango**
khào nǐaw màak muang ເຂົ້າໜຽວໝາກມ່ວງ

**sticky rice in coconut milk cooked in bamboo**
khào lǎam ເຂົ້າຫລາມ

**sweetened sticky rice steamed in banana leaves**
khào tôm ເຂົ້າຕົ້ມ

## drinks – non-alcoholic

ເຄື່ອງດື່ມທີ່ບໍ່ມີທາດເຫຼົ້າ

**water** ນ້ຳ

Drinking water (ນ້ຳດື່ມ, nâm deum) is purified for drinking purposes, whether boiled or otherwise treated. All water offered

to customers in restaurants or hotels will be purified so one needn't fret about the safety of taking a sip from a proffered glass or pitcher. In restaurants and most foodstalls, you can order nâm deum by the bottle, or you can ask for drinking water by the glass at no charge. The latter is usually drawn from 20L bottles of purified water or water boiled for drinking purposes.

| | | |
|---|---|---|
| **boiled water** | nâm tôm | ນ້ຳຕົ້ມ |
| **drinking water** | nâm deum | ນ້ຳດື່ມ |
| **ice** | nâm kâwn | ນ້ຳກ້ອນ |

### coffee & tea ກາເຟແລະນ້ຳຊາ

Good coffee is grown in the Bolaven Plateau area of Southern Laos. The Lao tend to brew coffee using pure coffee beans (rarely adding ground peanuts or chicory as in Thailand). Traditionally Lao coffee is roasted by wholesalers, ground by vendors and filtered just before serving. The typical Lao restaurant – especially those in hotels, guesthouses and other tourist-oriented establishments – serves instant coffee with packets of artificial, non-dairy creamer on the side.

If you want real Lao coffee ask for kạa-féh thŏng (ກາເຟຖົງ, bag coffee), or kạ-féh tôm (ກາເຟຕົ້ມ, boiled coffee), prepared by pouring hot water through a bag-shaped cloth filter containing ground coffee.

The Lao usually serve filtered coffee mixed with sugar. Some shops also add sweetened condensed milk. If you don't want sugar or milk, ask for kạa-féh dạm (ກາເຟດຳ, black coffee) and baw sai nâm-tạan (ບໍ່ໃສ່ນ້ຳຕານ, without sugar). Lao coffee usually comes in a small glass instead of a ceramic cup. Grasp the hot glass along the rim to avoid burnt fingers.

In Central and Southern Laos, coffee is almost always served with a chaser of hot nâm sáa (ນ້ຳຊາ, weak tea), while in the north it's typically served with a glass of plain hot water.

Chinese-style (green or semi-cured) teas predominate in Chinese and Vietnamese restaurants and are always served without sugar or milk. Black, Indian-style tea is typically found only in restaurants or foodstalls that serve Lao coffee. If you order sáa hâwn (ຊາຮ້ອນ, hot tea), it may arrive with sugar and condensed milk, so be sure to specify sáa dạm baw sai nâm-tạan

(ຊາດຳບໍ່ໃສ່ນ້ຳຕານ) if you prefer black tea without milk and/or sugar.

| | | |
|---|---|---|
| **hot water** | nâm hâwn | ນ້ຳຮ້ອນ |
| **cold water** | nâm yén | ນ້ຳເຢັນ |
| **hot Lao coffee with milk and sugar** | kąa-féh nóm hâwn | ກາເຟນົມຮ້ອນ |
| **hot Lao coffee with sugar, no milk** | kąa-féh dąm | ກາເຟດຳ |
| **hot Nescafé with milk and sugar** | naet nóm | ແນດນົມ |
| **hot Nescafé with sugar, no milk** | naet dąm | ແນດດຳ |
| **iced Lao coffee with sugar, no milk** | kąa-féh nóm yén | ກາເຟນົມເຢັນ |
| **iced Lao coffee with milk and sugar** | òh-lîang | ໂອລ້ຽງ |
| **weak tea** | nâm sáa | ນ້ຳຊາ |
| **hot Lao tea with sugar** | sáa hâwn | ຊາຮ້ອນ |
| **hot Lao tea with milk and sugar** | sáa nóm hâwn | ຊານົມຮ້ອນ |
| **iced Lao tea with milk and sugar** | sáa nóm yén | ຊານົມເຢັນ |
| **iced Lao tea with sugar, no milk** | sáa wǎan yén | ຊາຫວານເຢັນ |
| **no sugar** | baw sai nâm-tąan | ບໍ່ໃສ່ນ້ຳຕານ |
| **Ovaltine** | oh-wan-tin | ໂອວັນຕິນ |
| **orange juice (or orange soda)** | nâm màak kîang | ນ້ຳໝາກກ້ຽງ |
| **plain milk** | nâm nóm | ນ້ຳນົມ |
| **yogurt** | nóm sòm | ນົມສົ້ມ |

# drinks – alcoholic

ເຄື່ອງດື່ມທີ່ມີທາດເຫຼົ້າ

### beer

ເບຍ

Several kinds of beer are brewed by the Lao Brewery Company on the outskirts of Vientiane. Least expensive but very drinkable is LBC's draft beer (ເບຍສົດ, bịa sòt), which is only available in beer bars in Vientiane. LBC also bottles a Bia Lao (the French label reads Bière Larue) – look for the tiger's head on the label. In the northern provinces bordering China, various Chinese brands of beer are available – these generally cost less than Lao beer.

### distilled spirits

ເຫຼົ້າ

Rice whisky or lào láo (ເຫຼົ້າລາວ, Lao liquor) is a popular drink among lowland Lao. The government produces several brands which are very similar in taste to Thailand's famous 'Mekong whisky' and are best taken over ice with a splash of soda and a squeeze of lime.

In rural provinces, a weaker version of lào láo is fermented by households or villages. Strictly speaking, it's not legal but no-one seems to care. It's not always safe to drink, however, since unboiled water is often added during and after the fermentation process.

| | | |
|---|---|---|
| **beer** | bịa | ເບຍ |
| **draught beer** | bịa sót | ເບຍສົດ |
| **Lao rice whisky** | lào láo | ເຫຼົ້າລາວ |
| **soda water** | nâm sŏh-dạa | ນ້ຳໂສດາ |
| **glass** | jàwk | ຈອກ |
| **bottle** | kâew | ແກ້ວ |

| | | |
|---|---|---|
| Help! | suay dae | ຊ່ວຍແດ່ |
| It's an emergency! | súk sŏen | ສຸກເສີນ |
| Stop! | yút | ຢຸດ |
| Go away! | nĭi pại | ໜີໄປ |
| Watch out! | la-wáng | ລະວັງ |
| Thief! | khá-móhy (jọhn) | ຂະໂມຍ (ໂຈນ) |
| Fire! | fái mài | ໄຟໄໝ້ |

**There's been an accident!**
mĭi ú-bát-tí-het — ມີອຸບັດຕິເຫດ

**Call a doctor!**
suay ôen thaan mǎw hài dae — ຊ່ວຍເອີ້ນທ່ານໝໍໃຫ້ແດ່

**Call an ambulance!**
suay ôen lot hóhng mǎw dae — ຊ່ວຍເອີ້ນລົດໂຮງໝໍແດ່

**Call the police!**
suay ôen tam-lùat dae — ຊ່ວຍເອີ້ນຕຳຫລວດແດ່

**I've been robbed.**
khàwy thèuk khá-móhy — ຂ້ອຍຖືກຂະໂມຍ

**I've been raped.**
khàwy thèuk khòm khĕun — ຂ້ອຍຖືກຂົ່ມຂືນ

**I'll get the police.**
khàwy sii oên tam-lùat — ຂ້ອຍຊິເອີ້ນຕຳຫລວດ

## useful phrases

ປະໂຫຍກທີ່ເປັນປະໂຫຍດ

| | |
|---|---|
| **Could you help me please?**<br>jâo suay khàwy dâi baw | ເຈົ້າຊ່ວຍຂ້ອຍໄດ້ບໍ່ |
| **I am ill.**<br>khàwy puay | ຂ້ອຍປ່ວຍ |
| **I have health insurance.**<br>khàwy míi pá-kạn phái sú-khá-phâap | ຂ້ອຍມີປະກັນໄພ ສຸຂະພາບ |
| **My blood group is (A, B, O, AB) positive/negative.**<br>lêuat khàwy maen klúp (A, B, O, AB) bùak/lop | ເລືອດຂ້ອຍແມ່ນກຸລຸບ (A, B, O, AB) ບວກ/ລົບ |
| **I am lost.**<br>khàwy lǒng tháang | ຂ້ອຍຫລົງທາງ |
| **Where are the toilets?**<br>hàwng nâm yuu sǎi | ຫ້ອງນ້ຳຢູ່ໃສ |
| **Could I please use the telephone?**<br>sâi thóh-la-sáp dâi baw | ໃຊ້ໂທລະສັບໄດ້ບໍ່ |

SAFE TRAVEL

## police

ຕຳຫລວດ

**Where's the police station?**
sa-thǎa-níi tam-lùat yuu sǎi — ສະຖານີຕຳຫລວດຢູ່ໃສ

| | | |
|---|---|---|
| **My ... was/were stolen.** | ... khǎwng khàwy thèuk khá-móhy | ... ຂອງຂ້ອຍຖືກ ຂະໂມຍ |
| **I've lost my ...** | khàwy het ... sǐa lâew | ຂ້ອຍເຮັດ ... ເສຍແລ້ວ |
| **bags** | kọng kheuang | ຖົງເຄື່ອງ |
| **money** | ngóen | ເງິນ |
| **travellers cheques** | saek dọen tháang | ແຊັກເດີນທາງ |
| **passport** | nǎng-sěu phaan dạen | ໜັງສືຜ່ານ ແດນ |

**I would like to contact my embassy/consulate.**
yàak tít taw sa-thǎan-thûut khǎwng khàwy — ຢາກຕິດຕໍ່ສະຖານທູດ ຂອງຂ້ອຍ

**I speak (English).**
khàwy wâo pháa-sǎa (ạng-kít) — ຂ້ອຍເວົ້າພາສາ (ອັງກິດ)

**I understand.**
khàwy khào jại — ຂ້ອຍເຂົ້າໃຈ

**I don't understand.**
khàwy baw khào jại — ຂ້ອຍບໍ່ເຂົ້າໃຈ

**I didn't realise I was doing anything wrong.**
khàwy baw hûu dâi het nyǎng phít — ຂ້ອຍບໍ່ຮູ້ໄດ້ເຮັດ ຫຍັງຜິດ

**I didn't do it.**
khàwy baw dâi het ຂ້ອຍບໍ່ໄດ້ເຮັດ

**I'm sorry, I apologise.**
khăw thôht, sĭa jại ຂໍໂທດເສຍໃຈ

**My contact number in case of emergency (next of kin) is ...**
khâwp khúa thii já hài tít taw nái káw-la-níi súk sŏen ... ຄອບຄົວທີ່ຈະໃຫ້ຕິດຕໍ່ໃນກໍລະນີສຸກເສີນ ...

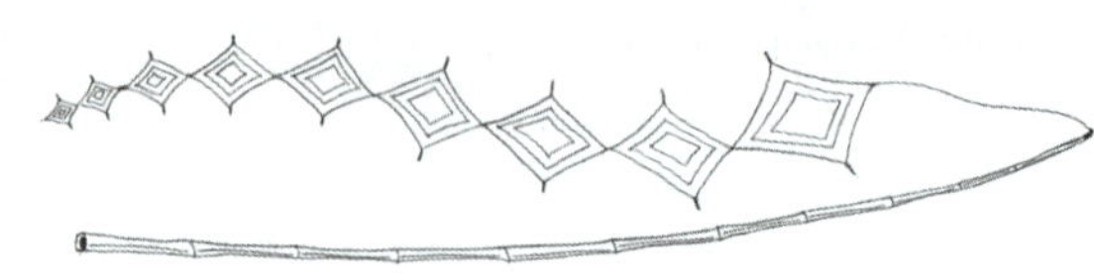

I need a ... — khàwy tâwng-kạan ... — ຂ້ອຍຕ້ອງການ ...
 dentist — mǎw pụa khàew — ໝໍປົວແຂ້ວ
 doctor — thaan mǎw — ທ່ານໝໍ

Where's the nearest ...? — ... yùu sǎi — ... ຢູ່ໃສ
 chemist — khóm bụng yáa — ຄົນປຸງຢາ
 hospital — hóhng mǎw — ໂຮງໝໍ

I'm sick.
 khàwy baw sá-bạai — ຂ້ອຍບໍ່ສະບາຍ

My friend is sick.
 pheuan khàwy baw sá-bạai — ເພື່ອນຂ້ອຍບໍ່ສະບາຍ

I need a doctor who speaks English.
 khàwy tâwng-kạan thaan mǎw hûu pháa-sǎa ạng-kít — ຂ້ອຍຕ້ອງການທ່ານໝໍຮູ້ພາສາອັງກິດ

Could the doctor come here?
 thaan mǎw máa nîi dâi baw — ທ່ານໝໍມານີ້ໄດ້ບໍ່

## women's health

ສຸຂະພາບແມ່ຍິງ

Could I see a female doctor?
 khàwy khǎw phop thaan mǎw phùu nyíng dâi baw — ຂ້ອຍຂໍພົບທ່ານໝໍຜູ້ຍິງໄດ້ບໍ່

I'm pregnant.
 khàwy thěu pháa-máan — ຂ້ອຍຖືພາມານ

I'm on the Pill.
 khàwy kịn yáa khúm — ຂ້ອຍກິນຢາຄຸມ

I haven't had my period for ... weeks.
 pá-jạm dẹuan khàwy baw máa dâi ... ạa-thit lâew — ປະຈຳເດືອນຂ້ອຍບໍ່ມາໄດ້ ... ອາທິດແລ້ວ

## ailments

ການເຈັບເປັນ

| | | |
|---|---|---|
| **I'm tired.** | khàwy meuay | ຂ້ອຍເໝື່ອຍ |
| **I'm not well.** | khàwy baw sá-bąai | ຂ້ອຍບໍ່ສະບາຍ |
| **I have a cold.** | pęn wát | ເປັນຫວັດ |
| **I have a fever.** | pęn khài | ເປັນໄຂ້ |
| **My stomach aches.** | pùat thâwng | ປວດທ້ອງ |
| **I have diarrhoea.** | lóng thâwng | ລົງທ້ອງ |
| **It hurts here.** | jép yuu nîi | ເຈັບຢູ່ນີ້ |
| **I can't sleep.** | náwn baw lap | ນອນບໍ່ລັບ |
| **My head aches.** | pùat hŭa | ປວດຫົວ |
| **My back hurts.** | pùat lăng | ປວດຫລັງ |

**There's pain in my chest.**
jép nàa óek — ເຈັບໜ້າເອິກ

**I have a sore throat.**
jép kháw — ເຈັບຄໍ

**I have vomited several times.**
hàak lăai theua — ຮາກຫລາຍເທື່ອ

**I have been like this for two weeks.**
pęn naew nîi dai săwng ąa-thit lâew — ເປັນແນວນີ້ໄດ້ສອງອາທິດແລ້ວ

**Is it serious?**
pęn nák baw — ເປັນໜັກບໍ່

| | | |
|---|---|---|
| **I feel ...** | khàwy hûu-séuk ... | ຂ້ອຍຮູ້ສຶກ ... |
| **dizzy** | įn hųa | ວິນຫົວ |
| **shivery** | năo son | ໜາວສັ່ນ |
| **weak** | awn phía | ອ່ອນເພຍ |

| | | |
|---|---|---|
| ache | pùat | ປວດ |
| AIDS | lôhk èht | ໂລກເອດສ |
| allergy | phâe | ແພ້ |
| anaemia | lôhk lêuat jạang | ໂລກເລືອດຈາງ |
| asthma | lôhk hèut | ໂລກຫືດ |
| blister | pẹn tum | ເປັນຕຸ່ມ |
| bronchitis | làwt lóm ák-sèhp | ຫລອດລົມອັກເສບ |
| burn | fái mâi | ໄຟໄໝ້ |
| cancer | ma-léhng | ມະເລງ |
| cholera | a-hí-wáa | ອະຫິວາ |
| cough | ại | ໄອ |
| cramps | pân (phùuk) | ປັ້ນ (ຜູກ) |
| dengue fever | khài lêuat àwk | ໄຂ້ເລືອດອອກ |
| diabetes | lôhk bạo wǎan | ໂລກເບົາຫວານ |
| diarrhoea | lóng thâwng | ລົງທ້ອງ |
| dysentery | lôhk thâwng bít | ໂລກທ້ອງບິດ |
| fever | khài | ໄຂ້ |

**they may say ...**

| | |
|---|---|
| pẹn nyǎng<br>What's the matter? | ເປັນຫຍັງ |
| jâo jép nyǎng baw<br>Do you feel any pain? | ເຈົ້າເຈັບຫຍັງບໍ່ |
| jép yuu sǎi<br>Where does it hurt? | ເຈັບຢູ່ໃສ |
| pẹn bàep nîi dọn<br>bạan-dại lâew<br>How long have you been like this? | ເປັນແບບນີ້ດົນ<br>ປານໃດແລ້ວ |
| jâo khóei pẹn bǎep nîi baw<br>Have you had this before? | ເຈົ້າເຄີຍເປັນແບບນີ້ບໍ່ |
| jâo kịn yáa baw<br>Are you on medication? | ເຈົ້າກິນຢາບໍ່ |
| jâo phâe ạn-dại baw<br>Are you allergic to anything? | ເຈົ້າແພ້ອັນໃດບໍ່ |
| jâo thěu pháa-máan baw<br>Are you pregnant? | ເຈົ້າຖືພາມານບໍ່ |

| | | |
|---|---|---|
| headache | pùat hŭa | ປວດຫົວ |
| heart condition | sá-phâap hŭa jại | ສະພາບຫົວໃຈ |
| hepatitis | tàp ák-sèhp | ຕັບອັກເສບ |
| infection | séum sêua | ຊຶມເຊື້ອ |
| inflammation | ák-sèhp | ອັກເສບ |
| influenza | khài wát nyai | ໄຂ້ຫວັດໃຫຍ່ |
| lice | tọh hăo | ໂຕເຫົາ |
| malaria | khài yúng | ໄຂ້ຍຸງ |
| migraine | jep hŭa háeng | ເຈັບຫົວແຮງ |
| pneumonia | lôhk pàwt bụam | ໂລກປອດບວມ |
| rabies | lôhk pẹn wâw | ໂລກເປັນບ້ |
| rash | tum | ຕຸ່ມ |
| sore throat | jep kháw | ເຈັບຄໍ |
| sprain | pùat khat | ປວດຂັດ |
| stomachache | pùat thâwng | ປວດທ້ອງ |
| sunburn | mâi dàet | ໄໝ້ແດດ |
| toothache | jép khàew | ເຈັບແຂ້ວ |
| veneral disease | kạm-ma lôhk | ກາມະໂລກ |

## parts of the body

ພາກສ່ວນຂອງຮ່າງກາຍ

| | | |
|---|---|---|
| arm | khăen | ແຂນ |
| back | lăng | ຫລັງ |
| breast | tâo nóm | ເຕົ້ານົມ |
| chest | óek | ເອິກ |
| ear | hŭu | ຫູ |
| eye | tạa | ຕາ |
| face | nàa | ໜ້າ |
| finger | nîu méu | ນີ້ວມື |
| foot/feet | tịin | ຕີນ |
| hand | méu | ມື |
| head | hŭa | ຫົວ |
| heart | hŭa jại | ຫົວໃຈ |
| jaw | kháang ká-tại | ຄາງກະໄຕ |
| kidney | màak khai lăng | ໝາກໄຂ່ຫລັງ |
| knee | hŭa khao | ຫົວເຂົ່າ |

| | | |
|---|---|---|
| leg | khăa | ຂາ |
| liver | táp | ຕັບ |
| lungs | pàwt | ປອດ |
| mouth | pàak | ປາກ |
| muscle | kâam sîin | ກ້າມຊີ້ນ |
| nose | dang | ດັງ |
| penis | a-wái-ya-wa | ອະໄວຍະວະ |
| | phêht sáai | ເພດຊາຍ |
| ribs | ká-dùuk khàang | ກະດູກຂ້າງ |
| shoulders | baa-lai | ບ່າໄລ່ |
| spine | ká-dùuk săn lăng | ກະດູກສັນຫລັງ |
| stomach | thâwng (ká-phaw) | ທ້ອງ (ກະເພາະ) |
| testicles | an-tha (hăm) | ອັນທະ (ຫຳ) |
| throat | kháw | ຄໍ |
| toe | nîu tiin | ນີ້ວຕີນ |
| tooth/teeth | khàew | ແຂ້ວ |
| vagina | sâwng khâwt | ຊ່ອງຄອດ |

## at the chemist

ຢູ່ຮ້ານຂາຍຢາ

| | | |
|---|---|---|
| antibiotics | yáa tâan sêua (sa-nit kin) | ຢາຕ້ານເຊື້ອ (ຊະນິດກິນ) |
| antiseptic | yáa tâan sêua (sa-nit tháa) | ຢາຕ້ານເຊື້ອ (ຊະນິດທາ) |
| aspirin | àet-sá-peh-lín | ແອສເປລິນ |
| Band-Aid (plaster) | phàa tít bàat | ຜ້າຕິດບາດ |
| bandage | phàa haw bàat | ຜ້າຫໍ່ບາດ |
| condom (latex) | thŏng yaang á-náa-mái | ຖົງຢາງອະນາໄມ |
| gauze | phàa kâw | ຜ້າກໍ່ |
| injection | sák yaa | ສັກຢາ |
| insulin | yaa kâe lôhk bao wăan | ຢາແກ້ໂລກ ເບົາຫວານ |
| morphine | máw-fíin | ມໍຟີນ |
| painkiller | yaa kâe pùat | ຢາແກ້ປວດ |
| pill/tablet | ya met | ຢາເມັດ |
| prescription | bai sang yaa | ໃບສັ່ງຢາ |

| | | |
|---|---|---|
| **sleeping medication** | yąa náwn láp | ຢານອນລັບ |
| **vitamin** | wi-tąa-mín | ວິຕາມິນ |

**I need something for ...**
khàwy tâwng-kąan ąn-dąi ąn neung pheua ... — ຂ້ອຍຕ້ອງການອັນໃດ ອັນໜຶ່ງເພື່ອ ...

**I have a prescription.**
khàwy míi bąi sang yáa — ຂ້ອຍມີໃບສັ່ງຢາ

**How many times a day?**
mêu-la ják theua — ມື້ລະຈັກເທື່ອ

**(Four) times a day.**
mêu-la (sii) theua — ມື້ລະ (ສີ່) ເທື່ອ

**How much per tablet/pill?**
láa kháa met-la thao dąi — ລາຄາເມັດລະເທົ່າໃດ

## useful words

ຄຳສັບທີ່ເປັນປະໂຫຍດ

| | | |
|---|---|---|
| **accident** | ú-bát-tí-hèht | ອຸບັດຕິເຫດ |
| **addict** | khón tít yąa | ຄົນຕິດຢາ |
| **allergic (to)** | phâe | ແພ້ |
| **ambulance** | lot hóhng mǎw | ລົດໂຮງໝໍ |
| **bite** | kát | ກັດ |
| **blood test** | kùat lêuat | ກວດເລືອດ |
| **blood** | lêuat | ເລືອດ |
| **bone** | ká-dùuk | ກະດູກ |
| **faint** | pęn lóm | ເປັນລົມ |
| **hospital** | hóhng mǎw | ໂຮງໝໍ |
| **ill** | puay | ປ່ວຍ |
| **inject** | sák yáa | ສັກຢາ |
| **itch** | khán | ຄັນ |
| **mentally ill** | sǐa jít | ເສຍຈິດ |
| **nurse** | náang pha-yáa-bąan | ນາງພະຍາບານ |
| **pain** | khwáam jép-pùat | ຄວາມເຈັບປວດ |
| **patient (n)** | khón jép | ຄົນເຈັບ |
| **pharmacy** | hâan khǎai yąa | ຮ້ານຂາຍຢາ |
| **pregnant** | thěu pháa-máan | ຖືພາມານ |

| | | |
|---|---|---|
| **skin** | phǐu nǎng | ຜິວໜັງ |
| **vitamins** | wi-tạa-mín | ວິຕາມິນ |
| **wound** | bàat phǎe (baat jép) | ບາດແຜ (ບາດເຈັບ) |

**I feel better/worse.**
khàwy hûu-séuk dị khêun/ jép-kwaa kao
ຂ້ອຍຮູ້ສຶກດີຂຶ້ນ/ເຈັບກວ່າເກົ່າ

**I've been vaccinated.**
khàwy dâi sák yáa pâwng kạn lâew
ຂ້ອຍໄດ້ສັກຢາປ້ອງກັນແລ້ວ

**I have high/low blood pressure.**
khàwy míi khwáam dạn lêuat sǔung/tam
ຂ້ອຍມີຄວາມດັນເລືອດສູງ/ຕ່ຳ

**I have my own syringe.**
khàwy míi sá-léng sak yáa suan tua
ຂ້ອຍມີສະແລັງສັກຢາສ່ວນຕົວ

| | | |
|---|---|---|
| I'm ... | khàwy pẹn ... | ຂ້ອຍເປັນ ... |
| diabetic | lôhk bạo wǎan | ໂລກເບົາຫວານ |
| asthmatic | lôhk héut | ໂລກຫືດ |
| anaemic | lôhk lêuat jạang | ໂລກເລືອດຈາງ |
| I'm allergic to ... | khàwy phâe ... | ຂ້ອຍແພ້ ... |
| antibiotics | yáa tâan sêua | ຢາຕ້ານເຊື້ອ |
| aspirin | áet-sá-pẹh-lín | ແອສເປລິນ |
| penicillin | pẹh-níi-síi-lín | ເປນີຊີລິນ |

## at the dentist

ຢູ່ທັນຕະແພດ

I have a toothache.
khàwy jép khàew — ຂ້ອຍເຈັບແຂ້ວ

I have a cavity.
khàwy pẹn khàew máeng — ຂ້ອຍເປັນແຂ້ວແມງ

I need a filling.
khàwy tâwng-kạan át khàew — ຂ້ອຍຕ້ອງການອັດແຂ້ວ

I've broken my tooth.
khàew khàwy tàek — ແຂ້ວຂ້ອຍແຕກ

My gums hurt.
khàwy jép hèuak — ຂ້ອຍເຈັບເຫືອກ

I don't want it extracted.
khàwy baw yàak lok khàew — ຂ້ອຍບໍ່ຢາກລົກແຂ້ວ

Please give me an anaesthetic.
suay sai yáa méun hài dae — ຊ່ວຍໃສ່ຢາມືນໃຫ້ແດ່

Ouch!
ọhy — ໂອຍ

SAFE TRAVEL

# SUSTAINABLE TRAVEL

With the scientific community no longer disputing the reality of climate change, the matter of sustainability becomes an important part of the travel vernacular. In practical terms, this means assessing our impact on the environment and local cultures and economies – and acting to make that impact as positive as possible. Here are some basic phrases to get you on your way …

## communication & cultural differences

**I'd like to learn some of your local dialects.**
khâwy yàak hien pháa-săa thâwng thin khăwng jâo
ຂ້ອຍຢາກຮຽນພາສາ ທ້ອງຖິ່ນຂອງເຈົ້າ

**Would you like me to teach you some English?**
jâo yàak hài khàwy săwn pháa-săa ąng-kit hài baw
ເຈົ້າຢາກໃຫ້ຂ້ອຍສອນ ພາສາອັງກິດໃຫ້ບໍ່

**Is this a local or national custom?**
nîi maen pá-phéh-nii khăwng thâwng thin lěu khăwng sâat
ນີ້ແມ່ນປະເພນີ ຂອງທ້ອງຖິ່ນ ຫຼືຂອງຊາດ

**I respect your customs.**
khâwy náp-thěu pá-phéh-nii khăwng jâo
ຂ້ອຍນັບຖື ປະເພນີຂອງເຈົ້າ

## community benefit & involvement

**What sorts of issues is this community facing?**
bạn-hăa nyăng thii thâwng thin nîi kạm-láng pá-sop
ບັນຫາຫຍັງທີ່ ທ້ອງຖິ່ນນີ້ ກຳລັງປະສົບ

| | | |
|---|---|---|
| **climate and monsoon weather** | phái thám-ma-sâat | ໄພທຳມະຊາດ |

| | | |
|---|---|---|
| deforestation | kạan tát-mâi | ການຕັດໄມ້ |
| freedom of the press | ít-sa-lá nái kạan khĭan khao săan | ອິສະລະໃນການ ຂຽນຂ່າວສານ |
| ongoing poverty | bạn-hăa khwáam nyâak jón | ບັນຫາ ຄວາມຍາກຈິນ |
| unemployment | kạan waang ngáan | ການຫວ່າງງານ |

**I'd like to volunteer my skills.**
khâwy yạak ạa-săa sá-mak hét wîek
ຂ້ອຍຢາກອາສາ ສະມັກເຮັດວຽກ

**Are there any volunteer programs available in the area?**
mii khóhng kạan ạa-săa-sa-mák yuu thâwng thin nîi baw
ມີໂຄງການ ອາສາສະມັກ ຢູ່ທ້ອງຖິ່ນນີ້ບໍ່

## environment

**Where can I recycle this?**
khâwy khwán thîm án nîi yuu săi
ຂ້ອຍຄວນຖິ້ມ ອັນນີ້ຢູ່ໃສ

## transport

**Can we get there by public transport?**
khii lót dawy sạan hâwt baw
ຂີ່ລົດໂດຍສານຮອດບໍ່

**Can we get there by bike?**
khii lot thìip hâwt baw
ຂີ່ລົດຖີບຮອດບໍ່

**I'd prefer to walk there.**
khâwy já nyaang ào
ຂ້ອຍຈະຍ່າງເອົາ

## accommodation

**I'd like to stay at a locally-run hotel.**
khâwy yạak phak yuu hóhng háem thii khón thâwng thin bạw-li-hăan
ຂ້ອຍຢາກພັກຢູ່ ໂຮງແຮມທີ່ຄົນ ທ້ອງຖິ່ນບໍລິຫານ

**Are there any ecolodges here?**
mii bawn phak nái khẹht
paa thám-ma-sâat baw
ມີບ່ອນພັກໃນເຂດ
ປ່າທຳມະຊາດບໍ່

**Can I turn the air conditioning off and open the window?**
khâwy yạak mâwt ạe yẹn
láe pŏet pawng yîam dâi baw
ຂ້ອຍຢາກມອດແອເຢັນ
ແລະເປີດປ່ອງຢ້ຽມໄດ້ບໍ່

**There's no need to change my sheets.**
baw tâwng píen phàa
pụu bawn
ບໍ່ຕ້ອງປ່ຽນຜ້າ
ປູບ່ອນ

## shopping

**Where can I buy locally produced goods/souvenirs?**
yuu săi thii khâwy săa-mâat
sêu khăwng sâi/
thii-la-léuk thii
khón thâwng thin hét
ຢູ່ໃສທີ່ຂ້ອຍສາມາດ
ຊື້ຂອງໃຊ້/
ທີ່ລະລຶກທີ່
ຄົນທ້ອງຖິ່ນເຮັດ

| | | |
|---|---|---|
| Is this made from ...? | nîi maen hét jạak ... baw | ນີ້ແມ່ນເຮັດ ຈາກ ... ບໍ່ |
| deer antlers | khăo kwạang | ເຂົາກວາງ |
| elephant tusks | ngáa sâang | ງາຊ້າງ |
| snake skin | năng ngúu | ຫນັງງູ |
| tiger skin | năng sĕua | ຫນັງເສືອ |

## food

| | | |
|---|---|---|
| Do you sell ...? | jâo khăai ... | ເຈົ້າຂາຍ ... |
| locally produced food | phá-lít-ta-phán ạa-hăan khăwng thâwng thin baw | ຜລິດຕະພັນ ອາຫານຂອງ ທ້ອງຖິ່ນບໍ່ |
| organic produce | phá-lít-ta-phán baw mii săan khéh-mii baw | ຜລິດຕະພັນ ບໍ່ມີສານ ເຄມີບໍ່ |

**Can you tell me which traditional foods I should try?**

| | |
|---|---|
| ạa-hǎan phêun méuang dǎi thii khâwy khwán síim | ອາຫານພື້ນເມືອງໃດ ທີ່ຂ້ອຍຄວນຊີມ |

## sightseeing

| | | |
|---|---|---|
| **Does your company ...?** | bạw-li-sát khǎwng thaan ... | ບໍລິສັດ ຂອງທ່ານ ... |
| **donate money to charity** | bạw-li-jàak ngóen hài sá-thǎan-thii sǒng kháw baw | ບໍລິຈາກ ເງິນໃຫ້ ສະຖານທີ່ ສົງເຄາະບໍ່ |
| **hire local guides** | jâang phûu nám thiaw jàak thâwng thin baw | ຈ້າງຜູ້ ນຳທ່ຽວຈາກ ທ້ອງຖິ່ນບໍ່ |
| **visit local businesses** | yîam yạam bán-dạa thú-la-kít thâwng thin baw | ຢ້ຽມຢາມ ບັນດາ ທຸລະກິດ ທ້ອງຖິ່ນບໍ້ |

| | | |
|---|---|---|
| **Does the guide speak ...?** | phûu nám thiaw wâo pháa-sǎa ... baw | ຜູ້ນຳທ່ຽວ ເວົ້າພາສາ ... ບໍ່ |
| **Karen** | ká-lieng | ກະຫລ່ຽງ |
| **Mong** | mông | ມົ້ງ |
| **Thaidam** | thái dạm | ໄທດຳ |
| **Vientiane** | láo wiéng-jạn | ລາວວຽງຈັນ |
| **Yao** | yâo | ຢ້າວ |

**Are cultural tours available?**

| | |
|---|---|
| mii kạan thawng thiaw wát-thá-ná-thám baw | ມີການທ່ອງທ່ຽວ ວັດທະນະທຳບໍ່ |

SUSTAINABLE TRAVEL

# A

| | | |
|---|---|---|
| to be able (can) | dâi | ໄດ້ |
| I can. | khàwy dâi | ຂ້ອຍໄດ້ |
| I can't. | khàwy baw dâi | ຂ້ອຍບໍ່ໄດ້ |
| Can you ...? | jâo dâi baw ... | ເຈົ້າໄດ້ບໍ່ ... |
| about (approximately) | pá-máan | ປະມານ |
| above (adv) | tháang thóeng | ທາງເທິງ |
| above (prep) | yuu thóeng | ຢູ່ເທິງ |
| abroad | taang pá-thêht | ຕ່າງປະເທດ |
| to accept | hap | ຮັບ |
| I accept. | khàwy hap | ຂ້ອຍຮັບ |
| Do you accept? | jâo hap baw | ເຈົ້າຮັບບໍ່ |
| accident | ú-bát-tí-hèht | ອຸບັດຕິເຫດ |
| accommodation | bawn phak | ບ່ອນພັກ |
| addiction | sèhp tít | ເສບຕິດ |
| address | thii yuu | ທີ່ຢູ່ |
| administration | kąan ját tâng | ການຈັດຕັ້ງ |
| admission (entry) | phaan khào | ຜ່ານເຂົ້າ |
| admission fee | khaa phaan pá-tųu | ຄ່າຜ່ານປະຕູ |
| to admit (allow entry) | á-nu-nyâat khào | ອະນຸຍາດເຂົ້າ |
| adult | phùu nyai | ຜູ້ໃຫຍ່ |

| | | |
|---|---|---|
| adventure | pá-jọn phái | ປະຈົນໄພ |
| aeroplane | héua bịn | ເຮືອບິນ |
| by aeroplane | dọhy héua bịn | ໂດຍເຮືອບິນ |
| after | lăng jàak | ຫຼັງຈາກ |
| again | ìik | ອີກ |
| against | tâan | ຕ້ານ |
| to agree | hĕn dịi | ເຫັນດີ |

| | | |
|---|---|---|
| I agree. | khàwy hĕn dịi | ຂ້ອຍເຫັນດີ |
| Do you agree? | jâo hĕn dịi baw | ເຈົ້າເຫັນດີບໍ່ |
| Agreed! | tók-lóng | ຕົກລົງ |

| | | |
|---|---|---|
| agriculture | ká-sí-kạm | ກະສິກຳ |
| ahead | kawn | ກ່ອນ |
| aid | suay lĕua | ຊ່ວຍເຫຼືອ |
| AIDS | lôhk èht | ໂລກເອດສ |
| airline | săai kạan bịn | ສາຍການບິນ |
| airmail | tháang ạa-kàat | ທາງອາກາດ |
| by airmail | dọhy tháang ạa-kàat | ໂດຍທາງອາກາດ |
| alarm clock | móhng púk | ໂມງປຸກ |
| all | tháng mót | ທັງໝົດ |
| allergy | phúum phâe | ພູມແພ້ |
| to allow | á-nu-mat | ອະນຸມັດ |
| almost | kèuap | ເກືອບ |
| alone | dòht diaw | ໂດດດ່ຽວ |
| also | khéu/teum | ຄື/ຕື່ມ |
| alternative | tháang lêuak | ທາງເລືອກ |
| always | lêuay lêuay | ເລື້ອຍໆ |
| amazing | ma-hat-sá-jạn | ມະຫັດສະຈັນ |
| ambassador | èhk-ák-kha-lat-thá-thûut | ເອກອັກຄະລັດຖະທູດ |
| ambulance | lot hóng măw | ລົດໂຮງໝໍ |
| among | la-waang | ລະຫວ່າງ |
| ancient | bọh-háan | ໂບຮານ |
| and | lae | ແລະ |

A

DICTIONARY

| | | |
|---|---|---|
| angry | hâai | ຮ້າຍ |
| antique (adj) | kheuang bọh-háan | ເຄື່ອງໂບຮານ |
| any | eun-dại | ອື່ນໃດ |
| anytime | wéh-láa dại kaw dâi | ເວລາໃດກໍ່ໄດ້ |
| apartment | ạa-kháan | ອາຄານ |
| appointment | kạan nat phop | ການນັດພົບ |
| approximately | pá-máan | ປະມານ |
| archaeological | bụu-háan-na-kha-dịi | ບູຮານນະຄະດີ |
| to argue | thók thĭang | ຖົກຖຽງ |
| argument | kạan thók thĭang | ການຖົກຖຽງ |
| to arrive | máa hâwt | ມາຮອດ |
| art | sĭi-la-pá | ສິລະປະ |
| to ask | thăam | ຖາມ |
| at (place) | yuu thii | ຢູ່ທີ່ |
| at (time) | nái wéh-láa | ໃນເວລາ |
| automatic | ọh-tọh-nóh-mat | ໂອໂຕໂນມັດ |

# B

| | | |
|---|---|---|
| baby | dék nâwy | ເດັກນ້ອຍ |
| back | lăng | ຫລັງ |
| backpack | bạa-lóh; thŏng pêh | ບ໋າໂລ; ຖົງເປ້ |
| bad | sua | ຊົ່ວ |
| bag | kheuang/thŏng | ເຄື່ອງ/ຖົງ |
| baggage | ká-pạo kheuang | ກະເປົາເຄື່ອງ |
| ball (object) | màak bạan | ໝາກບານ |
| bank | tha-náa-kháan | ທະນາຄານ |
| bar | bạa | ບາ |
| to bathe | àap nâm | ອາບນ້ຳ |
| bathers (swimsuit) | sut láwy nâm | ຊຸດລອຍນ້ຳ |
| women's | khăwng mae nyíng | ຂອງແມ່ຍິງ |
| men's | khăwng phùu sáai | ຂອງຜູ້ຊາຍ |
| bathroom | hàwng nâm | ຫ້ອງນ້ຳ |
| battery | thaan fái săai; mâw fái | ຖ່ານໄຟສາຍ; ໝໍ້ໄຟ |
| beautiful | ngáam | ງາມ |
| because | phaw-waa | ເພາະວ່າ |

| | | |
|---|---|---|
| bed | tịang | ຕຽງ |
| before (conj) | kawn | ກອນ |
| before (prep) | kawn | ກ່ອນ |
| beggar | khón khăw tháan | ຄົນຂໍທານ |
| to begin | loem | ເລີ່ມ |
| beginner | phùu loem tôn | ຜູ້ເລີ່ມຕົ້ນ |
| behind | tháang lăng | ທາງຫລັງ |
| below (adv) | yuu lum | ຢູ່ລຸ່ມ |
| below (prep) | bêuang lum | ເບື້ອງລຸ່ມ |
| beside | khàang káp | ຂ້າງກັບ |
| best | dịi thii-sút | ດີທີ່ສຸດ |
| better | dịi kwaa | ດີກ່ວາ |
| between (prep) | la-waang | ລະຫວ່າງ |
| Bible | tạm-láa săa-sa-náa khlit | ຕຳລາສາສະນາຄລິດ |
| bicycle | lot thìip | ລົດຖີບ |
| big | nyai | ໃຫຍ່ |
| bill | bại bịin | ໃບບິນ |
| birthday | wán kòet | ວັນເກີດ |
| to bite | kát | ກັດ |
| bitter | khŏm | ຂົມ |
| blanket | phàa hom | ຜ້າຫົ່ມ |
| to bless | ụay pháwn | ອ່ວຍພອນ |
| blind | tạa bàwt | ຕາບອດ |
| blood | lêuat | ເລືອດ |
| boat | héua | ເຮືອ |
| bomb | la-bòet | ລະເບີດ |

| | | |
|---|---|---|
| **Bon appetit!** | sóen sâep | ເຊີນແຊບ |

| | | |
|---|---|---|
| book | pêum | ປຶ້ມ |
| bookshop | hâan khăai pêum | ຮ້ານຂາຍປຶ້ມ |
| border | sáai dạen | ຊາຍແດນ |

| | | |
|---|---|---|
| **bored** | beua naai | ເບື່ອໜ່າຍ |
| **I'm bored.** | khàwy beua | ຂ້ອຍເບື່ອ |

| | | |
|---|---|---|
| to borrow | yéum | ຢືມ |
| **May I borrow this?** | khǎw yéum dae | ຂໍຢືມແດ່ |
| boss | náai | ນາຍ |
| both | tháng sǎwng | ທັງສອງ |
| bottle opener | kheuang khǎi kâew | ເຄື່ອງໄຂແກ້ວ |
| boy | dék sáai | ເດັກຊາຍ |
| brake(s) | hàam | ຫ້າມ |
| bread | khào jii | ເຂົ້າຈີ່ |
| to break | tàek | ແຕກ |
| breakfast | ąa-hǎan sâo | ອາຫານເຊົ້າ |
| to breathe | hǎai jai | ຫາຍໃຈ |
| bribe | sǐn bọn | ສິນບົນ |
| to bribe | hài sǐn bọn | ໃຫ້ສິນບົນ |
| bridge | khǔa | ຂົວ |
| bright | jâeng | ແຈ້ງ |
| to bring | ąo máa | ເອົາມາ |
| **Can you bring it?** | jâo ąo máa dâi baw | ເຈົ້າເອົາມາໄດ້ບໍ່ |
| broken | phéh lâew | ເພແລ້ວ |
| bucket | khú sai nâm | ຊຸໃສ່ນ້ຳ |
| building | ąa-kháan | ອາຄານ |
| to burn | jút/mâi | ຈູດ/ໄໝ້ |
| bus | lot méh | ລົດເມ |
| business | thu-la-kít | ທຸລະກິດ |
| busy | kháa wîak; nyùng | ຄາວຽກ; ຫຍຸ້ງ |
| but | tae waa | ແຕ່ວ່າ |

| | | |
|---|---|---|
| to buy | sêu | ຊື້ |
| Where did you buy this? | jâo sêu nîi máa tae sǎi | ເຈົ້າຊື້ນີ້ມາແຕ່ໃສ |



# C

| | | |
|---|---|---|
| Cafe | hâan kạa-féh | ຮ້ານກາເຟ |
| camera | kâwng thaai hûup | ກ້ອງຖ່າຍຮູບ |
| to camp | tâng khêm | ຕັ້ງເຕັ້ມ |
| can (tin) | ká-pạwng | ກະປອງ |
| can | dâi | ໄດ້ |
| Can I take a photograph? | thaai hûup dâi baw | ຖ່າຍຮູບໄດ້ບໍ່ |
| No, you can't. | baw dâi | ບໍ່ໄດ້ |

| | | |
|---|---|---|
| cancel | yok lôek | ຍົກເລີກ |
| can opener | kheuang khǎi ká-pạwng | ເຄືອງໄຂກະປອງ |
| candle | thían | ທຽນ |
| capital (city) | na-kháwn lǔang | ນະຄອນຫລວງ |
| capitalism | théun-ni-nyom | ທຶນນິຍົມ |
| car | lot | ລົດ |
| cards (playing) | phâi | ໄພ້ |
| to care | dụu-láe | ດູແລ |
| I don't care. | khàwy baw sǒn | ຂ້ອຍບໍ່ສົນ |
| Careful! | la-wáng | ລະວັງ |

| | | |
|---|---|---|
| to carry | ạo máa | ເອົາມາ |
| I'll carry it. | khàwy já ạo máa | ຂ້ອຍຈະເອົາມາ |

| | | |
|---|---|---|
| CD | phaen síi-dịi | ແຜ່ນຊີດີ |
| to celebrate | sá-lǎwng | ສະຫລອງ |
| cemetery | paa sâa | ປ່າຊ້າ |
| certificate | bại yang-yéun | ໃບຢັ້ງຢືນ |
| certain (sure) | nae náwn | ແນ່ນອນ |

| | | |
|---|---|---|
| Are you certain? | jâo nae jại baw | ເຈົ້າແນ່ໃຈບໍ່ |

| | | |
|---|---|---|
| chair | tang nang | ຕັ່ງນັ່ງ |
| chance | ọh-kàat | ໂອກາດ |
| by chance | dọhy bạng ọen | ໂດຍບັງເອີນ |
| change (money) | ngóen nâwy | ເງິນນ້ອຍ |
| cheap | thèuk | ຖືກ |
| cheese | nóei | ເນີຍ |
| chemist | phùu khǎai yáa | ຜູ້ຂາຍຢາ |
| child | dék nâwy | ເດັກນ້ອຍ |
| chocolate | khào-nǒm sóh-kọh-laet | ເຂົ້າໜົມໂຊໂກແລັດ |
| to choose | lêuak | ເລືອກ |
| church | bòht khlit | ໂບດຄລິດ |
| cigarettes | yáa sùup | ຢາສູບ |
| cinema | hóng hûup ngáo | ໂຮງຮູບເງົາ |
| city | méuang | ເມືອງ |
| city centre | jại káang méuang | ໃຈກາງເມືອງ |
| clean (adj) | khwáam sá-àat | ຄວາມສະອາດ |
| close (nearby) | kâi | ໃກ້ |
| to close | át/pít | ອັດ/ປິດ |

| | | |
|---|---|---|
| It's closed. | pít lâew | ປິດແລ້ວ |

| | | |
|---|---|---|
| clothing | kheuang nung | ເຄື່ອງນຸ່ງ |
| coin | ngóen lǐan | ເງິນຫລຽນ |
| cold (adj; climate) | nǎo | ໜາວ |
| cold (n) | khwáam nǎo | ຄວາມໜາວ |
| colour | sǐi | ສີ |
| to come | máa | ມາ |

| | | |
|---|---|---|
| comfortable | sá-bạai | ສະບາຍ |
| communism | la-bàwp khàwm-múu-nit | ລະບອບຄອມມູນິດ |
| company (business) | bạw-li-sat | ບໍລິສັດ |
| complex (adj) | nyùng nyěuangz | ຫຍຸ້ງເຫຍືອງ |
| condom | thǒng yáang á-náa-mái | ຖົງຢາງອະນາໄມ |
| to confirm | yéun yán | ຢືນຢັນ |

| | | |
|---|---|---|
| Congratulations! | sóm sóei | ຊົມເຊີຍ |

| | | |
|---|---|---|
| constipation | nyeung thâwng | ຍຶ່ງທ້ອງ |
| consulate | kọng-sǔun | ກົງສູນ |
| contact lens | waen sai kâew tạa | ແວ່ນໃສ່ແກ້ວຕາ |
| contagious | pha-nyâat tít-taw | ພະຍາດຕິດຕໍ່ |
| contraceptive | sing khúm kạm-nôet | ສິ່ງຄຸມກຳເນີດ |
| conversation | kạan sǒn-tha-náa | ການສົນທະນາ |
| to cook | taeng kịn | ແຕ່ງກິນ |
| corner (of a room) | jạe hâwng | ແຈຫ້ອງ |
| corner (of a street) | tháang nyâek | ທາງແຍກ |
| at/on the corner | yuu tháang nyâek | ຢູ່ທາງແຍກ |
| corrupt (adj) | kịn sǐn bọn | ກິນສິນບົນ |
| corruption | kạan kịn sǐn bọn | ການກິນສິນບົນ |
| cost | láa-kháa | ລາຄາ |
| to cost | míi láa-kháa | ມີລາຄາ |

| | | |
|---|---|---|
| It costs ... | mán míi láa-kháa | ມັນມີລາຄາ ... |
| How much does it cost? | láa-kháa thao dại | ລາຄາເທົ່າໃດ |

| | | |
|---|---|---|
| to cough | ại | ໄອ |
| to count | nap | ນັບ |
| crazy | bâa | ບ້າ |
| credit card | bát khréh-dit | ບັດຄເຣດິດ |
| crop | phǒn-la-pùuk | ຜົນລະປູກ |
| cross (angry) | khîat khâen | ຄຽດແຄ້ນ |

| | | |
|---|---|---|
| customs office | hàwng-kạan | ຫ້ອງການພາສີ |
| | pháa-sĭi ạa-kạwn | ອາກອນ |
| to cut | tát | ຕັດ |
| to cycle | khii lot thìip | ຂີ່ລົດຖີບ |

# D

| | | |
|---|---|---|
| dad | phaw | ພໍ່ |
| daily | pá-jạm wán | ປະຈຳວັນ |
| damp | jêun | ຈື້ນ |
| to dance | fâwn | ຟ້ອນ |
| dangerous | ạn-ta-láai | ອັນຕະລາຍ |
| dark | mêut | ມືດ |
| date (time) | wán thíi | ວັນທີ |
| date of birth | wán kòet | ວັນເກີດ |
| dawn | ạa-lún | ອາລຸນ |
| day | kạang wén | ກາງເວັນ |
| dead | tạai lâew | ຕາຍແລ້ວ |
| deaf | hŭu nùak | ຫູໜວກ |
| death | khwáam tạai | ຄວາມຕາຍ |
| to decide | tát sĭn jại | ຕັດສິນໃຈ |
| decision | kạan tát sĭn jại | ການຕັດສິນໃຈ |
| delay | jó | ໂຈະ |
| delicious | sâep | ແຊບ |
| delightful | muan seun | ມ່ວນຊື່ນ |
| democracy | pá-sáa-thi-pá-tại | ປະຊາທິປະໄຕ |
| demonstration (protest) | kạan dọen khá-bụan | ການເດີນຂະບວນ |
| to depart (leave) | àwk | ອອກ |

| | | |
|---|---|---|
| The flight departs at ... | thìaw bịn àwk ... | ຖ້ຽວບິນອອກ ... |
| What time does it leave? | àwk ják móhng | ອອກຈັກໂມງ |

| | | |
|---|---|---|
| department store | hâan sap-pha-sĭn-khâa | ຮ້ານຊັບພະສິນຄ້າ |
| departure | kạan àwk | ການອອກ |

| | | |
|---|---|---|
| to destroy | thám láai | ທຳລາຍ |
| development | kąan phat-tha-náa | ການພັດທະນາ |
| diabetes | lôhk bąo-wǎan | ໂລກເບົາຫວານ |
| dictionary | pêum wat-já-náa-nu-kǫm | ປຶ້ມວັດຈະນານຸກົມ |
| different | tàek-taang | ແຕກຕ່າງ |
| difficult | nyàak | ຫຍາກ |

| | | |
|---|---|---|
| It's difficult. | nyùng nyàak | ຫຍຸ້ງຍາກ |

| | | |
|---|---|---|
| dinner | ąa-hǎan láeng | ອາຫານແລງ |
| direct | dǫhy kǫng | ໂດຍກົງ |
| direction (adv) | thit tháang | ທິດທາງ |
| dirt | dįn | ດິນ |
| dirty | pêuan | ເປື້ອນ |
| disabled person | khón phi-kąan | ຄົນພິການ |
| discount | lut láa-kháa | ລຸດລາຄາ |
| discrimination | kąan jąm-nâek | ການຈຳແນກ |
| disinfectant | yáa khàa sêua | ຢາຂ້າເຊື້ອ |
| distant | kąi | ໄກ |
| to do | het | ເຮັດ |

| | | |
|---|---|---|
| I'll do it. | khàwy síi het | ຂ້ອຍຊິເຮັດ |
| Can you do that? | jâo het dâi baw | ເຈົ້າເຮັດໄດ້ບໍ່ |
| Don't do it. | yáa het | ຢ່າເຮັດ |

| | | |
|---|---|---|
| doctor | thaan mǎw | ທ່ານໝໍ |
| dog | mǎa | ໝາ |
| doll | hun | ຮຸ່ນ |
| door | pá-tųu | ປະຕູ |
| double | khuu | ຄູ່ |
| double bed | tįang khuu | ຕຽງຄູ່ |
| double room | hàwng khuu | ຫ້ອງຄູ່ |
| down | lum | ລຸ່ມ |

D

DICTIONARY

| | | |
|---|---|---|
| **downtown** | kạang méuang | ກາງເມືອງ |
| **dream** | khwáam fǎn | ຄວາມຝັນ |
| **to dream** | fǎn | ຝັນ |
| **to dress** | nung | ໜຸ່ງ |
| **dried** | hàeng | ແຫ້ງ |
| **drink** | kheuang deum | ເຄື່ອງດື່ມ |

| | | |
|---|---|---|
| **I don't drink spirits.** | khàwy baw kịn lào | ຂ້ອຍບໍ່ກິນເຫຼົ້າ |
| **Do you drink beer?** | jâo kịn bịa baw | ເຈົ້າກິນເບຍບໍ |

| | | |
|---|---|---|
| **to drink** | deum | ດື່ມ |
| **drinkable** | pẹn tạa deum | ເປັນຕາດື່ມ |
| **drinkable water** | nâm deum | ນ້ຳດື່ມ |
| **to drive** | kháp | ຂັບ (ລົດ) |
| **drivers licence** | bại á-nu-nyâat kháp-khii | ໃບອະນຸຍາດຂັບຂີ່ |
| **drugs (illegal)** | yáa sèhp tít | ຢາເສບຕິດ |
| **drunk (inebriated)** | máo lào | ເມົາເຫຼົ້າ |
| **dry (adj)** | hàeng | ແຫ້ງ |
| **during** | la-waang | ລະຫວ່າງ |
| **dust** | khìi fun | ຂີ້ຝຸ່ນ |

# E

| | | |
|---|---|---|
| **each** | tae-la | ແຕ່ລະ |
| **early** | tae sâo | ແຕ່ເຊົ້າ |
| **to earn** | dâi | ໄດ້ |
| **earnings** | láai hap | ລາຍຮັບ |
| **Earth** | nuay lôhk | ໜ່ວຍໂລກ |
| **earthquake** | phaen-dịn wǎi | ແຜ່ນດິນໄຫວ |
| **east** | thit tạa-wén àwk | ທິດຕາເວັນອອກ |
| **easy** | ngaai | ງ່າຍ |
| **to eat** | kịn | ກິນ |
| **economical** | pá-yat | ປະຢັດ |

| | | |
|---|---|---|
| economics | sèht-thá-sàat | ເສດຖະສາດ |
| economy | sèht-thá-kít | ເສດຖະກິດ |
| economy (thrift) | kaan pá-yat | ການປະຢັດ |
| education | kaan séuk-sǎa | ການສຶກສາ |
| elections | kaan lêuak tâng | ການເລືອກຕັ້ງ |
| electricity | fái fâa | ໄຟຟ້າ |
| elevator (lift) | lip (khân dai fái fâa) | ລິບ (ຂັ້ນໄດໄຟຟ້າ) |
| email | ii-máew | ອີແມວ |
| embassy | sá-thǎan thûut | ສະຖານທູດ |
| emergency exit | tháang àwk súk sǒen | ທາງອອກສຸກເສີນ |
| employer | náai jâang | ນາຍຈ້າງ |
| empty | pao | ເປົ່າ |
| end | jóp | ຈົບ |
| energy | pha-láng-ngáan | ພະລັງງານ |
| English | pháa-sǎa ang-kít | ພາສາອັງກິດ |
| to enjoy (oneself) | muan | ມ່ວນ |
| enough | phaw | ພໍ |
| to enter | khào | ເຂົ້າ |
| entrance | tháang khào | ທາງເຂົ້າ |
| entry | kaan-khào | ການເຂົ້າ |
| environment | sing wâet-lâwm | ສິ່ງແວດລ້ອມ |
| equal (adj) | thao káp | ເທົ່າກັບ |
| European (person) | khón yúu-lôhp | ຄົນຢູໂລບ |
| evening | tawn khám | ຕອນຄ່ຳ |
| event | ngáan thêht-sá-kaan | ງານເທດສະການ |
| every | thuk-thuk/tae-la | ທຸກໆ/ແຕ່ລະ |
| every day | thuk wán | ທຸກວັນ |
| everyone | thuk khón | ທຸກຄົນ |
| everything | thuk yaang | ທຸກຢ່າງ |
| example | tua yaang | ຕົວຢ່າງ |
| for example | yok tua yaang | ຍົກຕົວຢ່າງ |
| to exchange | lâek pian | ແລກປ່ຽນ |

| | | |
|---|---|---|
| Excuse me. | khǎw thôht | ຂໍໂທດ |

| | | |
|---|---|---|
| **exhausted** | meuay | ເໝື່ອຍ |
| **exhibition** | wáang sá-dạeng | ວາງສະແດງ |
| **exile** | phùu theuk néh-la-thêht | ຜູ້ຖືກເນລະເທດ |
| **to exile** | néh-la-thêht | ເນລະເທດ |
| **exit** | tháang àwk | ທາງອອກ |
| **expensive** | pháeng | ແພງ |
| **experience** | pá-sóp-kạan | ປະສົບການ |
| **export** | sĭn-khâa song àwk | ສິນຄ້າສົ່ງອອກ |
| **to export** | song àwk sĭn-khâa | ສົ່ງອອກສິນຄ້າ |
| **eye** | tạa | ຕາ |

# F

| | | |
|---|---|---|
| **false (wrong)** | phít | ຜິດ |
| **false (fake)** | pạwm | ປອມ |
| **family** | khâwp khúa | ຄອບຄົວ |
| **fan (cooling)** | phat lóm | ພັດລົມ |
| **fan (sports)** | khăa khĭa | ຂາເຊຍ |
| **far** | kại | ໄກ |
| **farm** | bawn phá-lit ká-sí-kạm | ບ່ອນຜະລິດກະສິກຳ |
| **fast (adj)** | wái | ໄວ |
| **to fast** | ngot kịn ạa-hăan | ງົດກິນອາຫານ |
| **fat (adj)** | tûi | ຕຸ້ຍ |
| **fat** | khăi mán | ໄຂມັນ |
| **father** | phaw | ພໍ່ |
| **fault** | khwáam phít phâat | ຄວາມຜິດພາດ |

| | | |
|---|---|---|
| **It's my fault.** | khwáam phít khăwng khàwy | ຄວາມຜິດຂອງຂ້ອຍ |

| | | |
|---|---|---|
| **fear** | khwáam yâan | ຄວາມຢ້ານ |
| **fee** | láa-kháa | ລາຄາ |
| **to feel** | hûu-séuk | ຮູ້ສຶກ |
| **feeling** | khwáam-hûu-séuk | ຄວາມຮູ້ສຶກ |
| **ferry** | héua dọhy-săan | ເຮືອໂດຍສານ |
| **festival** | ngáan bụn | ງານບຸນ |
| **fever** | khài | ໄຂ້ |

| | | |
|---|---|---|
| few | nàwy | ໜ້ອຍ |
| a few | nàwy dịaw | ໜ້ອຍດຽວ |
| fiance(e) | khuu màn | ຄູ່ໝັ້ນ |
| film (movie) | hûup ngáo | ຮູບເງົາ |
| film (roll of) | fím thaai hûup | ຟີມຖ່າຍຮູບ |
| filtered (water) | nâm kạwng | ນ້ຳ ກອງ |
| fine (penalty) | páp măi | ປັບໃໝ |
| fire | fái | ໄຟ |
| firewood | féun | ຟືນ |
| first | thii neung | ທີໜຶ່ງ |
| fish | pạa | ປາ |
| flag | thúng | ທຸງ |
| flashlight (torch) | fái săai | ໄຟສາຍ |
| flight | thìaw bịn | ຖ້ຽວບິນ |
| flood | ú-thok-ká-phái | ອຸທົກກະໄພ |
| floor | phêun | ພື້ນ |
| on the floor | yuu phêun | ຢູ່ພື້ນ |
| flower(s) | dàwk mâi | ດອກໄມ້ |
| to follow | tạam | ຕາມ |

| | | |
|---|---|---|
| Follow me! | tạam khàwy | ຕາມຂ້ອຍ |

| | | |
|---|---|---|
| food | ạa-hăan | ອາຫານ |
| food poisoning | ạa-hăan pẹn phít | ອາຫານເປັນພິດ |
| football (soccer) | bạan-té | ບານເຕະ |
| foreign | taang pá-thêht | ຕ່າງປະເທດ |
| foreigner | khón taang pá-thêht | ຄົນຕ່າງປະເທດ |
| forever | tá-làwt kạan | ຕະຫລອດການ |
| to forget | léum | ລືມ |

| | | |
|---|---|---|
| I forgot. | khàwy léum | ຂ້ອຍລືມ |

| | | |
|---|---|---|
| to forgive | hài ạ-phái | ໃຫ້ອະໄພ |
| formal | tháang kạan | ທາງການ |

F

DICTIONARY

| | | |
|---|---|---|
| fragile | kheuang tàek ngaai | ເຄື່ອງແຕກງ່າຍ |
| free (gratis) | hài lâa | ໃຫ້ລ້າ |
| free (not bound) | ít-sá-la | ອິດສະລະ |
| to freeze | sae khăeng | ແຊ່ແຂງ |
| fresh | sót | ສົດ |
| friend | pheuan | ເພື່ອນ |
| friendly | pheuan mitt | ເພື່ອນມິດ |
| full | tẹm | ເຕັມ |
| fun | muan | ມ່ວນ |
| funny | tá-lók | ຕະຫຼົກ |

# G

| | | |
|---|---|---|
| game | kạan lìin | ການຫຼິ້ນ |
| garbage | khìi yèua | ຂີ້ເຫຍື້ອ |
| garden | sŭan | ສວນ |
| gas (cooking) | ạai kàet | ອາຍແກັສ |
| gas (petrol) | nâm-mán àet-sáng | ນ້ຳມັນແອັດຊັງ |
| gate | pá-tụu | ປະຕູ |
| generous | êua-fêua | ເອື້ອເຟື້ອ |
| gift | khăwng khwăn | ຂອງຂວັນ |
| girl | dék nyíng | ເດັກຍິງ |
| girlfriend | fáen (nyíng) | ແຟນ(ຍິງ) |
| to give | ạo hâi | ເອົາໃຫ້ |

| | | |
|---|---|---|
| Give me ... | ạo hâi dae ... | ເອົາໃຫ້ແດ່ ... |
| I'll give you ... | já ạo hâi jâo ... | ຈະເອົາໃຫ້ເຈົ້າ ... |

| | | |
|---|---|---|
| glass (drinking) | jàwk | ຈອກ |
| glasses (spectacles) | waen tạa | ແວ່ນຕາ |
| to go (on foot) | pại (nyaang) | ໄປ (ຍ່າງ) |

| | | |
|---|---|---|
| I'm going to ... (do something) | khàwy já ... | ຂ້ອຍຈະ ... |
| I'm going to ... (somewhere) | khàwy já pại ... | ຂ້ອຍຈະໄປ ... |
| Are you going there? | jâo sii pại hàn baw | ເຈົ້າຊິໄປຫັ້ນບໍ່ |

| | | |
|---|---|---|
| **God** | pha-jâo | ພະເຈົ້າ |
| **good** | dịi | ດີ |
| **government** | lat-thá-bạan | ລັດຖະບານ |
| **greedy** | mak dâi | ມັກໄດ້ |
| **to grow (increase)** | khá-nyǎai | ຂະຫຍາຍ |
| **to grow (produce)** | pùuk | ປູກ |
| **to guess** | dạo | ເດົາ |
| **guide** | pha-nak-ngạan nám thiaw | ພະນັກງານນຳທ່ຽວ |
| **guidebook** | pêum nám thiaw | ປຶ້ມນຳທ່ຽວ |
| **guilty** | ká-thám phít | ກະທຳຜິດ |
| **guitar** | kí-tạa | ກີຕາ |

# H

| | | |
|---|---|---|
| **hair** | phǒm | ຜົມ |
| **hairdresser** | saang sǒem sǔay | ຊ່າງເສີມສວຍ |
| **half** | khoeng | ເຄິ່ງ |
| **handbag** | ká-pạo hìu | ກະເປົາຫິ້ວ |
| **handicapped person** | khón phi-kạan | ຄົນພິການ |
| **handicrafts** | hát-thá-kạm | ຫັດຖະກຳ |
| **handsome** | ngáam | ງາມ |
| **happy** | dịi-jại | ດີໃຈ |

| | | |
|---|---|---|
| **Happy Birthday!** | súk-sǎn wán kòet | ສຸກສັນວັນເກີດ |

| | | |
|---|---|---|
| **hard (difficult)** | nyàak | ຍາກ |
| **hard (not soft)** | khǎeng | ແຂງ |
| **to hate** | sáng | ຊັງ |
| **to have** | míi | ມີ |

| | | |
|---|---|---|
| **I have ...** | khàwy míi ... | ຂ້ອຍມີ ... |
| **You have ...** | jào míi ... | ເຈົ້າມີ ... |
| **Do you have ...?** | jâo míi ... baw | ເຈົ້າມີ ... ບໍ່ |

| | | |
|---|---|---|
| he | láo | ລາວ |
| health | sú-khá-phâap | ສຸຂະພາບ |
| health centre | sǔun á-náa-mái | ສູນອະນາໄມ |
| to hear | dâi-nyín | ໄດ້ຍິນ |
| heat | khwáam hâwn | ຄວາມຮ້ອນ |
| heater | kheuang het hài un | ເຄື່ອງເຮັດໃຫ້ອຸ່ນ |
| heavy | nák | ໜັກ |
| hello | sá-bạai dịi | ສະບາຍດີ |
| help | khwáam suay lěua | ຄວາມຊ່ວຍເຫຼືອ |

| | | |
|---|---|---|
| Can I help (you)? | míi nyǎng hài suay baw | ມີຫຍັງໃຫ້ຊ່ວຍບໍ່ |
| Help! | sûay dae | ຊ່ວຍແດ່ |

| | | |
|---|---|---|
| to help | suay | ຊ່ວຍ |
| here | yuu nîi | ຢູ່ນີ້ |
| high | sǔung | ສູງ |
| hill | phúu | ພູ |
| to hire (someone) | jâang | ຈ້າງ |

| | | |
|---|---|---|
| I'd like to hire him. | khàwy yàak jâang láo | ຂ້ອຍຢາກຈ້າງລາວ |

| | | |
|---|---|---|
| to hire (rent) | sao | ເຊົ່າ |

| | | |
|---|---|---|
| I'd like to hire it. | khàwy yàak sao | ຂ້ອຍຢາກເຊົ່າ |

| | | |
|---|---|---|
| holiday (religious) | wán bụn | ວັນບຸນ |
| holiday (vacation) | wán phak wîak | ວັນພັກວຽກ |
| on holiday | pại thiaw | ໄປທ່ຽວ |
| school holidays | wán phak hían | ວັນພັກຮຽນ |
| holy | sák-sít | ສັກສິດ |
| home | héuan | ເຮືອນ |
| homeland | ma-tú-phúum | ມະຕຸພູມ |

| | | |
|---|---|---|
| homosexual (adj) | mak phêht dịaw-kạn | ມັກເພດດຽວກັນ |
| homosexual | khón mak phêht dịaw-kạn | ຄົນມັກເພດດຽວກັນ |
| honest | seu-sát | ຊື່ສັດ |
| hope | khwáam wǎng | ຄວາມຫວັງ |
| to hope | wǎng | ຫວັງ |
| hospital | hóhng mǎw | ໂຮງໝໍ |
| hospitality | kạan tâwn hap | ການຕ້ອນຮັບ |
| hot | hâwn | ຮ້ອນ |
| hot (weather) | ạa-kàat hâwn | ອາກາດຮ້ອນ |
| hot (spicy) | phét | ເຜັດ |
| hotel | hóhng háem | ໂຮງແຮມ |
| hotel room | hàwng phak hóhng háem | ຫ້ອງພັກໂຮງແຮມ |
| house | héuan | ເຮືອນ |
| housework | wîak heuan | ວຽກເຮືອນ |
| how | náew-dại | ແນວໃດ |

| | | |
|---|---|---|
| How do I get to ...? | khàwy já pại hâwt ... dâi náew-dại | ຂ້ອຍຈະໄປຮອດ ... ໄດ້ແນວໃດ |
| How are you? | jâo sá-bại dịi baw ... | ເຈົ້າສະບາຍດີບໍ່ ... |
| How much is/are ...? | láa-kháa thao dại ... | ລາຄາເທົ່າໃດ ... |

| | | |
|---|---|---|
| human | ma-nut | ມະນຸດ |
| hungry | hǐu khào | ຫິວເຂົ້າ |

| | | |
|---|---|---|
| I'm hungry. | khàwy hǐu khào | ຂ້ອຍຫິວເຂົ້າ |
| Are you hungry? | jâo hǐu khào baw | ເຈົ້າຫິວເຂົ້າບໍ |

| | | |
|---|---|---|
| to hurry | fâo | ຟ້າວ |
| to hurt | jép | ເຈັບ |
| husband | phǔa | ຜົວ |

# I

| | | |
|---|---|---|
| I | khàwy | ຂ້ອຍ |
| ice | nâm kâwn | ນ້ຳກ້ອນ |
| with ice | sai nâm kâwn | ໃສ່ນ້ຳກ້ອນ |
| without ice | baw sai nâm kâwn | ບໍ່ໃສ່ນ້ຳກ້ອນ |
| ice cream | ká-láen | ກະແລັມ |
| icon | ąa-nu-sǎwn | ອານຸສອນ |
| idea | náew khwáam khít | ແນວຄວາມຄິດ |
| identification | bát pá-jạm tụa | ບັດປະຈຳຕົວ |
| if | thàa waa | ຖ້າວ່າ |
| ill | khài | ໄຂ້ |
| illegal | phít kót-mǎai | ຜິດກົດໝາຍ |
| imagination | jín-tá-náa-kạan | ຈິນຕະນາການ |
| imitation | khǎwng pạwm | ຂອງປອມ |
| immediately | thán thíi | ທັນທີ |
| import | sǐn khâa khǎa khào | ສິນຄ້າຂາເຂົ້າ |
| to import | kạan nám khào | ການນຳເຂົ້າ |
| important | sǎm-khán | ສຳຄັນ |
| impossible | pẹn pại baw dâi | ເປັນໄປບໍ່ໄດ້ |
| imprisonment | tít khuk | ຕິດຄຸກ |
| in | nái | ໃນ |
| included | pá-kàwp dûay | ປະກອບດ້ວຍ |
| inconvenient | baw sá-dùak | ບໍ່ສະດວກ |
| industry | út-sǎa-há-kạm | ອຸດສາຫະກຳ |
| infectious | tít sêua | ຕິດເຊື້ອ |
| infection | kạan tít sêua | ການຕິດເຊື້ອ |
| informal | baw pẹn tháang kạan | ບໍ່ເປັນທາງການ |
| information | khàw múun | ຂໍ້ມູນ |
| injection | kạan sák yáa | ການສັກຢາ |
| injury | bàat jép | ບາດເຈັບ |
| insect repellent | yáa kạn máeng mâi | ຢາກັນແມງໄມ້ |
| inside | pháai nái | ພາຍໃນ |
| insurance | pá-kạn phái | ປະກັນໄພ |
| to insure | pá-kạn | ປະກັນ |

| | | |
|---|---|---|
| It's insured. | pá-kạn lâew | ປະກັນແລ້ວ |

| | | |
|---|---|---|
| intelligent | sá-làat | ສະຫລາດ |
| interested | sǒn-jại | ສົນໃຈ |
| interesting | pẹn tạa sǒn-jại | ເປັນຕາສົນໃຈ |
| international | la-waang sâat | ລະຫວ່າງຊາດ |
| Internet | ịn-tọe-naet | ອິນເຕີແນັດ |
| Internet cafe | ịn-tọe-naet kạa-féh | ອິນເຕີແນັດກາເຟ |
| invitation | bát sóen | ບັດເຊີນ |

# J

| | | |
|---|---|---|
| jail | khuk | ຄຸກ |
| jazz | tọn-tịi jàet | ດົນຕີແຈສ |
| jeans | sòng yíin | ສົ້ງຢີນ |
| jewellery | kheuang pá-dáp | ເຄື່ອງປະດັບ |
| job | wîak | ວຽກ |
| joke | khwáam yâwk | ຄວາມຢອກ |

| | | |
|---|---|---|
| I'm joking. | khàwy wâo yâwk | ຂ້ອຍເວົ້າຢອກ |

| | | |
|---|---|---|
| journey | dọen tháang | ເດີນທາງ |
| juice (fruit) | nâm màak mâi | ນ້ຳໝາກໄມ້ |
| justice | khwáam nyu-tí-thám | ຄວາມຍຸຕິທຳ |

# K

| | | |
|---|---|---|
| key | ká-jạe | ກະແຈ |
| to kill | khàa | ຂ້າ |
| kind | jại dịi | ໃຈດີ |
| king | jâo síi-wit | ເຈົ້າຊີວິດ |
| kiss | kạan jùup | ການຈູບ |
| to kiss | jùup | ຈູບ |
| knapsack | bạa-lóh | ບາໂລ |
| to know (a person) | hûu-ják | ຮູ້ຈັກ |
| to know (something) | hûu | ຮູ້ |

| | | |
|---|---|---|
| I know him. | khàwy hûu-ják láo | ຂ້ອຍຮູ້ຈັກລາວ |

# L

| | | |
|---|---|---|
| lake | năwng | ໜອງ |
| land | phaen dịn | ແຜ່ນດິນ |
| landslide | dịn thá-lom | ດິນຖະຫລົ່ມ |
| language | pháa-săa | ພາສາ |
| large | kwâang/nyai | ກ້ວາງ/ໃຫຍ່ |
| last (in a series) | sút-thâai | ສຸດທ້າຍ |
| last (as in 'last week') | kawn | ກ່ອນ |
| late | sâa | ຊ້າ |

| | | |
|---|---|---|
| I'm late! | khàwy máa sâa | ຂ້ອຍມາຊ້າ |

| | | |
|---|---|---|
| to be late | máa sâa | ມາຊ້າ |
| later | tạwn lăng | ຕອນຫລັງ |
| to laugh | hŭa | ຫົວ |

| | | |
|---|---|---|
| Don't laugh! | yaa hŭa | ຢ່າຫົວ |

| | | |
|---|---|---|
| laundry (washing) | sak kheuang | ຊັກເຄື່ອງ |
| laundry (place) | hóhng sak kheuang | ໂຮງຊັກເຄື່ອງ |
| law | kót-măai | ກົດໝາຍ |
| lawyer | nak kót-măai | ນັກກົດໝາຍ |
| lazy | khâan | ຄ້ານ |
| to learn | hían | ຮຽນ |

I want to learn Lao.
khàwy yàak hían pháa-săa láo — ຂ້ອຍຢາກຮຽນພາສາລາວ

| | | |
|---|---|---|
| to leave (depart) | àwk; àwk jàak | ອອກ; ອອກຈາກ |

| | | |
|---|---|---|
| The flight leaves at ... | thìaw bịn àwk wéh-láa ... | ຖ້ຽວບິນອອກເວລາ ... |
| What time does the bus leave? | lot méh àwk ják móhng | ລົດເມອອກຈັກໂມງ |
| We're leaving for Vientiane tonight. | khéun nîi phûak háo já àwk pại wíeng jạn | ຄືນນີ້ພວກເຮົາຈະ ອອກໄປວຽງຈັນ |

| | | |
|---|---|---|
| to leave (behind) | pá-wâi | ປະໄວ້ |
| lecturer | wi-tha-nyáa-kạwn | ວິທະຍາກອນ |
| left (not right) | bêuang sâi | ເບື້ອງຊ້າຍ |
| on/to the left | tháang sâi | ທາງຊ້າຍ |
| legal | thèuk kót-mǎai | ຖືກກົດໝາຍ |
| less | nàwy-kwaa | ໜ້ອຍກວ່າ |
| letter | jót-mǎai | ຈົດໝາຍ |
| liar | khón khìi tua | ຄົນຂີ້ຕົວະ |
| lice | hǎo | ເຫົາ |
| life | síi-wit | ຊີວິດ |
| lift (elevator) | lip (khân dại fái fâa) | ລິບ (ຂັ້ນໄດໄຟຟ້າ) |
| light (not heavy) | bạo | ເບົາ |
| light | fái | ໄຟ |
| lighter (cigarette) | káp fái | ກັບໄຟ |
| like (similar) | khéu | ຄື |
| to like | mak | ມັກ |

| | | |
|---|---|---|
| I like ... | khàwy mak ... | ຂ້ອຍມັກ ... |
| Do you like ...? | jâo mak ... baw | ເຈົ້າມັກ ... ບໍ່ |

| | | |
|---|---|---|
| line | sèn seu | ເສັ້ນຊື່ |
| to listen | fáng | ຟັງ |

| | | |
|---|---|---|
| Listen to me. | fáng khàwy | ຟັງຂ້ອຍ |

| | | |
|---|---|---|
| **little (dimension)** | nàwy | ໜ້ອຍ |
| **little (quantity)** | nàwy | ໜ້ອຍ |
| **to live** | ạa-săi yuu | ອາໄສຢູ່ |

| | | |
|---|---|---|
| **I live in ...** | khàwy yuu ... | ຂ້ອຍຢູ່ ... |
| **Where do you live?** | jâo yuu săi | ເຈົ້າຢູ່ໃສ |

| | | |
|---|---|---|
| **local** | thâwng thin | ທ້ອງຖິ່ນ |
| **lock** | lái/kạwn | ໄລ/ກອນ |
| **long** | nyáo | ຍາວ |
| **long ago** | tae dọn | ແຕ່ດົນ |
| **to look** | boeng | ເບິ່ງ |
| **to look for** | sâwk hăa | ຊອກຫາ |
| **to lose** | sĭa | ເສຍ |
| **to lose (one's way)** | lŏng tháang | ຫຼົງທາງ |

| | | |
|---|---|---|
| **I'm lost.** | khàwy lŏng tháang | ຂ້ອຍຫລົງທາງ |

| | | |
|---|---|---|
| **lost (adj, things)** | sĭa hăai | ເສຍຫາຍ |

| | | |
|---|---|---|
| **I've lost my money.** | khàwy het ngóen sĭa | ຂ້ອຍເຮັດເງິນເສຍ |

| | | |
|---|---|---|
| **loud** | dạng | ດັງ |
| **love** | khwáam hak | ຄວາມຮັກ |
| **to love (be fond of)** | mak | ມັກ |
| **to love (relationships)** | hak | ຮັກ |

| | | |
|---|---|---|
| **I love you.** | khàwy hak jâo | ຂ້ອຍຮັກເຈົ້າ |

| | | |
|---|---|---|
| **luck** | sôhk | ໂຊກ |
| **lucky** | míi sôhk | ມີໂຊກ |
| **luggage** | ká-pạo | ກະເປົາ |
| **lunch** | ạa-hăan thiang | ອາຫານທ່ຽງ |

# M

| | | |
|---|---|---|
| machine | kheuang ják | ເຄື່ອງຈັກ |
| mad (crazy) | bâa | ບ້າ |
| made (of) | phá-lit dọhy | ຜະລິດໂດຍ |
| mail | jot-măai | ຈົດໝາຍ |
| main | săm-khán | ສຳຄັນ |
| majority | suan nyai | ສ່ວນໃຫຍ່ |
| to make | het | ເຮັດ |

| | | |
|---|---|---|
| Did you make it? | jâo het baw | ເຈົ້າເຮັດບໍ່ |

| | | |
|---|---|---|
| man | phùu sáai | ຜູ້ຊາຍ |
| many | lăai | ຫຼາຍ |
| map | phăen-thii | ແຜນທີ່ |
| market | ta-làat | ຕະຫລາດ |
| at the market | yuu ta-làat | ຢູ່ຕະຫລາດ |
| marriage | kạan taeng-ngáan | ການແຕ່ງງານ |
| to marry | taeng-ngáan | ແຕ່ງງານ |

| | | |
|---|---|---|
| I'm married. | khàwy taeng-ngáan lâew | ຂ້ອຍແຕ່ງງານແລ້ວ |

| | | |
|---|---|---|
| massage | nûat | ນວດ |
| matches | káp-khìit | ກັບຂີດ |
| maybe | bạang thii | ບາງທີ |
| medicine | yáa | ຢາ |
| to meet (someone) | phop | ພົບ |

| | | |
|---|---|---|
| I'll meet you. | khàwy já phop jâo | ຂ້ອຍຈະພົບເຈົ້າ |

| | | |
|---|---|---|
| to meet (each other) | phop kạn | ພົບກັນ |

| | | |
|---|---|---|
| Let's meet! | phop kạn thaw | ພົບກັນເທາະ |

| | | |
|---|---|---|
| menu | láai-kạan ạa-hǎan | ລາຍການອາຫານ |
| message | khàw-khwáam | ຂໍ້ຄວາມ |
| milk | nâm nóm | ນ້ຳນົມ |
| million | lâan | ລ້ານ |
| mind | jít jại | ຈິດໃຈ |
| to mind (to object) | baw hěn dịi | ບໍ່ເຫັນດີ |

| | | |
|---|---|---|
| Do you mind ...? | ... pẹn nyǎng baw | ... ເປັນຫຍັງບໍ່ |
| Never mind! | baw pẹn nyǎng | ບໍ່ເປັນຫຍັງ |

| | | |
|---|---|---|
| mineral water | nâm háe thâat | ນ້ຳແຮທາດ |
| minute | náa-thii | ນາທີ |
| to miss (someone) | khit hâwt | ຄິດຮອດ |
| mistake | khwáam phít | ຄວາມຜິດ |
| to make a mistake | het phít | ເຮັດຜິດ |

| | | |
|---|---|---|
| You've made a mistake. | jâo het phít | ເຈົ້າເຮັດຜິດ |

| | | |
|---|---|---|
| to mix | pá-sǒm kạn | ປະສົມກັນ |
| modern | thán sá-mǎi | ທັນສະໄໝ |
| money | ngóen | ເງິນ |
| month | dẹuan | ເດືອນ |
| monument | á-nu-sǎa-wa-líi | ອະນຸສາວະລີ |
| more (of something) | ìik | ອີກ |
| morning | tạwn sâo | ຕອນເຊົ້າ |
| mountain | phúu dạwy | ພູດອຍ |
| mountain-climbing | khèun phúu | ຂຶ້ນພູ |
| mother | mae | ແມ່ |
| movie | hûup ngáo | ຮູບເງົາ |

| | | |
|---|---|---|
| Let's see a movie. | pại boeng hûup ngáo | ໄປເບິ່ງຮູບເງົາ |

| | | |
|---|---|---|
| museum | phi-phit-tha-phán | ພິພິດທະພັນ |

| | | |
|---|---|---|
| music | dọn-tịi | ດົນຕີ |
| musician | nak-dọn-tịi | ນັກດົນຕີ |

# N

| | | |
|---|---|---|
| name | seu | ຊື່ |

| | | |
|---|---|---|
| My name is ... | khàwy seu ... | ຂ້ອຍຊື່ ... |
| What's your name? | jâo seu nyǎng | ເຈົ້າຊື່ຫຍັງ |

| | | |
|---|---|---|
| national park | sǔan út-thi-nyáan | ສວນອຸດທິຍານ |
| nature | thám-ma-sâat | ທຳມະຊາດ |
| near (prep) | kâi | ໄກ້ |
| nearby | yuu kâi | ຢູ່ໄກ້ |
| necessary | jạm-pẹn | ຈຳເປັນ |
| need | tâwng-kạan | ຕ້ອງການ |

| | | |
|---|---|---|
| I need ... | khàwy tâwng-kạan ... | ຂ້ອຍຕ້ອງການ ... |
| We need ... | háo tâwng-kạan ... | ເຮົາຕ້ອງການ ... |

| | | |
|---|---|---|
| neither ... nor | baw ... lěu | ບໍ່ ... ຫຼື |
| never | baw khóei | ບໍ່ເຄີຍ |
| new | mai | ໃໝ່ |
| news | khao | ຂ່າວ |
| newspaper | nǎng-sěu phím | ໜັງສືພິມ |
| next | taw pại | ຕໍ່ໄປ |
| night | khám | ຄ່ຳ |
| no | baw | ບໍ່ |
| noise | sǐang dạng | ສຽງດັງ |
| noisy | song sǐang dạng | ສົ່ງສຽງດັງ |
| north | něua | ເໜືອ |
| nothing | baw míi nyǎng | ບໍ່ມີຫຍັງ |
| not yet | nyáng | ຍັງ |
| now | dịaw-nîi | ດຽວນີ້ |

# O

| | | |
|---|---|---|
| obvious | thii hûu kạn dịi | ທີ່ຮູ້ກັນດີ |
| occupation | ạa-sîip | ອາຊີບ |
| ocean | ma-hăa-sá-mut | ມະຫາສະມຸດ |
| to offend | luang kọen | ລ່ວງເກີນ |
| to offer | ạo hài | ເອົາໃຫ້ |
| office | hàwng kạan | ຫ້ອງການ |
| often | sá-mam sá-mŏe | ສະໝ່ຳສະເໝີ |
| oil (petroleum) | nâm-mán | ນ້ຳມັນ |
| oil (vegetable) | nâm-mán phêut | ນ້ຳມັນພືດ |
| OK | tók-lóng | ຕົກລົງ |
| old | kae/thâo | ແກ/ເຖົ້າ |
| Olympic Games | kí-láa ọh-láem-pík | ກິລາໂອແລມປິກ |
| on (location) | yuu thóeng | ຢູ່ເທິງ |
| on (a particular day) | thii | ທີ່ |
| once | theua dịaw | ເທື່ອດຽວ |
| once more | ìik theua neung | ອີກເທື່ອໜຶ່ງ |
| once (upon a time) | tae kawn | ແຕ່ກ່ອນ |
| one | neung | ໜຶ່ງ |
| one-way | thìaw dịaw | ທ້ຽວດຽວ |
| only | thao-nân | ເທົ່ານັ້ນ |
| open (adj) | pòet | ເປີດ |
| opinion | khwáam khit-hĕn | ຄວາມຄິດເຫັນ |

| | | |
|---|---|---|
| In my opinion ... | tạam khwáam khit khàwy... | ຕາມຄວາມຄິດຂ້ອຍ... |

| | | |
|---|---|---|
| opportunity | ọh-kàat | ໂອກາດ |
| opposite (adj) | tàek taang | ແຕກຕ່າງ |
| opposite (prep) | kọng kạn khàam | ກົງກັນຂ້າມ |
| or | lĕu | ຫຼື |
| order | khám-sang | ຄຳສັ່ງ |
| to order | sang | ສັ່ງ |
| ordinary | thám-ma-dạa | ທຳມະດາ |
| organisation | ọng-kạan ját tâng | ອົງການຈັດຕັ້ງ |
| to organise | ját | ຈັດ |

| | | |
|---|---|---|
| original | tôn sá-báp | ຕົ້ນສະບັບ |
| other | eun | ອື່ນ |
| outside | tháang-nâwk | ທາງນອກ |
| over (prep) | yuu thóeng | ຢູ່ເທິງ |
| overnight | háem khéun | ແຮມຄືນ |
| overseas | taang pá-thêht | ຕ່າງປະເທດ |
| to owe | tít-nìi | ຕິດໜີ້ |

| | | |
|---|---|---|
| I owe you. | khàwy tít nìi jâo | ຂ້ອຍຕິດໜີ້ເຈົ້າ |
| You owe me. | jâo tít nìi khàwy | ເຈົ້າຕິດໜີ້ຂ້ອຍ |

| | | |
|---|---|---|
| owner | jâo khăwng | ເຈົ້າຂອງ |

# P

| | | |
|---|---|---|
| pack (of cigarettes) | sáwng (yáa sùup) | ຊອງ (ຢາສູບ) |
| package | haw | ຫໍ່ |
| packet | sáwng | ຊອງ |
| padlock | ká-jạe | ກະແຈ |
| painful | jép | ເຈັບ |
| painkillers | yáa kâe pùat | ຢາແກ້ປວດ |
| painting | hûup tâem | ຮູບແຕ້ມ |
| pair | khuu | ຄູ່ |
| palace | wáng | ວັງ |
| paper | jîa | ເຈ້ຍ |
| parcel | kheuang fàak | ເຄື່ອງຝາກ |
| parents | phaw mae | ພໍ່ແມ່ |
| park | sŭan săa-tháa-la-na | ສວນສາທາລະນະ |
| parliament | sá-pháa phùu tháen | ສະພາຜູ້ແທນ |
| part | phâak suan | ພາກສ່ວນ |
| to participate | míi suan huam | ມີສ່ວນຮ່ວມ |
| participation | kạan khào huam | ການເຂົ້າຮ່ວມ |
| party (fiesta) | ngáan pạa-tị | ງານປາຕີ |
| party (political) | phak kạan méuang | ພັກການເມືອງ |
| passenger | phùu dọhy-săan | ຜູ້ໂດຍສານ |
| passport | năng-sĕu phaan dạen | ໜັງສືຜ່ານແດນ |

| | | |
|---|---|---|
| path | tháang nyaang | ທາງຍ່າງ |
| to pay | jaai | ຈ່າຍ |
| peace | săn-tí-phâap | ສັນຕິພາບ |
| people (crowd) | fŭung són | ຝູງຊົນ |
| people (nation) | pá-sáa-són | ປະຊາຊົນ |
| perfect (adj) | sŏm-buun | ສົມບູນ |
| permanent | thăa-wáwn | ຖາວອນ |
| permission | kaan á-nu-mat | ການອະນຸມັດ |
| with your permission | á-nu-mat jàak jâo | ອະນຸມັດຈາກເຈົ້າ |
| permit | bai á-nu-nyâat | ໃບອະນຸຍາດ |
| to permit | á-nu-nyâat | ອະນຸຍາດ |
| persecution | kaan lóng thôht | ການລົງໂທດ |
| person | khón | ຄົນ |
| personal | suan tua | ສ່ວນຕົວ |
| personality | ní-săi | ນິໄສ |
| petrol | nâm-mán àet-sáng | ນ້ຳມັນແອັດຊັງ |
| pharmacy | hâan khăai yáa | ຮ້ານຂາຍຢາ |
| phone book | pêum thóh-la-sáp | ປຶ້ມໂທລະສັບ |
| photograph | hûup thaai | ຮູບຖ່າຍ |
| to photograph | thaai hûup | ຖ່າຍຮູບ |

| | | |
|---|---|---|
| Can I take a photograph? | khàw thaai hûup dâi baw | ຂ້ອຍຖ່າຍຮູບໄດ້ບໍ່ |

| | | |
|---|---|---|
| piece | pìang | ປ່ຽງ |
| place | bawn | ບ່ອນ |
| plant | phêut | ພືດ |
| plate | jaan | ຈານ |
| play (theatre) | la-kháwn | ລະຄອນ |
| to play | lìn | ຫຼິ້ນ |

| | | |
|---|---|---|
| Please. | ká-lu-náa | ກະລຸນາ |

| | | |
|---|---|---|
| plenty | lăai | ຫຼາຍ |

P

english–lao

| | | |
|---|---|---|
| poetry | ká-wíi | ກະວີ |
| to point (with one's finger) | sîi méu | ຊີ້ມື |
| police | tạm-lùat | ຕຳຫລວດ |
| politics | kạan-méuang | ການເມືອງ |
| pollution | món-la-phit | ມົນລະພິດ |
| pool (swimming) | sa láwy nâm | ສະລອຍນ້ຳ |
| poor | thuk-jọn | ທຸກຈົນ |
| port | thaa héua | ທ່າເຮືອ |
| positive (certain) | nae jại | ແນ່ໃຈ |

| | | |
|---|---|---|
| I'm positive. | khàwy nae jại | ຂ້ອຍແນ່ໃຈ |

| | | |
|---|---|---|
| postage stamp | sá-tạem | ສະແຕມ |
| postcard | bát pại-sá-níi | ບັດໄປສະນີ |
| post code | la-hát pại-sá-níi | ລະຫັດໄປສະນີ |
| post office | hàwng-kạan pại-sa-níi | ຫ້ອງການໄປສະນີ |
| pottery (items) | kheuang pân dịn phǎo | ເຄື່ອງປັ້ນດິນເຜົາ |
| pottery (place) | bawn phá-lit kheuang pân dịn phǎo | ບ່ອນຜະລິດເຄື່ອງປັ້ນດິນເຜົາ |
| poverty | khwáam thuk-jọn | ຄວາມທຸກຈົນ |
| power (strength) | pha-láng | ພະລັງ |
| power (political) | ạm-nâat | ອຳນາດ |
| practical | sing thii pẹn pại dâi | ສິ່ງທີ່ເປັນໄປໄດ້ |
| prayer | khám á-thi-thǎan | ຄຳອະທິຖານ |
| to prefer | mák | ມັກ |

| | | |
|---|---|---|
| I prefer ... | khàwy mák ... | ຂ້ອຍມັກ ... |

| | | |
|---|---|---|
| pregnant | thěu pháa | ຖືພາ |
| present (now) | pá-jú-bạn | ປະຈຸບັນ |
| present (gift) | khǎwng khwǎn | ຂອງຂວັນ |
| president | pá-tháan pá-thêht | ປະທານປະເທດ |
| pretty | ngáam | ງາມ |

| | | |
|---|---|---|
| prevent | pâwng-kạn | ປ້ອງກັນ |
| price | láa-kháa | ລາຄາ |
| priest | khún phaw | ຄຸນພໍ່ |
| prime minister | náa-yok | ນາຍົກ |
| prison | khuk | ຄຸກ |
| prisoner | nak-thôht | ນັກໂທດ |
| private | èh-ká-són | ເອກະຊົນ |
| probably | àat-já | ອາດຈະ |
| problem | pạn-hǎa | ປັນຫາ |
| procession | khá-bụan | ຂະບວນ |
| to produce | phá-lit | ຜະລິດ |
| professional | méu ạa-sîip | ມືອາຊີບ |
| profit | kạm-lái | ກຳໄລ |
| promise | kạan sǎn-nyáa | ການສັນຍາ |
| to promise | sǎn-nyáa | ສັນຍາ |
| prostitute | sǒh-phéh-níi | ໂສເພນີ |
| to protect | pâwng-kạn | ປ້ອງກັນ |
| protest | kạan pá-thûang | ການປະທ້ວງ |
| to protest | pá-thûang | ປະທ້ວງ |
| public | khǎwng sǎa-tháa-la-na | ຂອງສາທາລະນະ |
| public (adj) | sǎa-tháa-la-na | ສາທາລະນະ |
| in public | bawn sǎa-tháa-la-na | ບ່ອນສາທາລະນະ |
| to pull | dẹung | ດຶງ |
| to push | nyûu | ຍູ້ |
| to put | wáang/sai | ວາງ/ໃສ່ |

# Q

| | | |
|---|---|---|
| quality | khún-na-phâap | ຄຸນນະພາບ |
| of good quality | khún-na-phâap dịi | ຄຸນນະພາບດີ |
| question | khám thǎam | ຄຳຖາມ |
| queue | khíu/thǎew | ຄິວ/ແຖວ |
| quick (adj) | wái | ໄວ |
| quickly | wái | ໄວ |
| quiet (adj) | ngîap | ງຽບ |

# R

| | | |
|---|---|---|
| race (contest) | kạan khaeng-khăn | ການແຂ່ງຂັນ |
| racist | khón jạm-nâek phǐu phán | ຄົນຈຳແນກຜິວພັນ |
| radio | wi-tha-nyu | ວິທະຍຸ |
| railway | tháang lot fái | ທາງລົດໄຟ |
| by rail | dọhy lot fái | ໂດຍລົດໄຟ |
| rain | fŏn | ຝົນ |

| | | |
|---|---|---|
| It's raining. | fŏn tók | ຝົນຕົກ |

| | | |
|---|---|---|
| rape | kha-dịi khom khĕun | ຄະດີຂົ່ມຂືນ |
| to rape | khom khĕun | ຂົ່ມຂືນ |
| rare (unusual) | hăa nyàak | ຫາຍາກ |
| raw | díp | ດິບ |
| razor blades | bại-mîit thăe | ໃບມີດແຖ |
| to read | aan | ອ່ານ |
| ready | phâwm lâew | ພ້ອມແລ້ວ |
| reason | săa-het | ສາເຫດ |
| receipt | bại hap ngóen | ໃບຮັບເງິນ |
| recently | ạa-dìit phaan pại baw dọn | ອາດີດຜ່ານໄປບໍ່ດົນ |
| to recommend | nae-nám | ແນະນຳ |
| refrigerator | tûu yén | ຕູ້ເຢັນ |
| refugee | óp-pha-nyop | ອົບພະຍົບ |
| refund | tháen khéun | ແທນຄືນ |
| refuse | khìi nyèua | ຂີ້ເຫຍື້ອ |
| to refuse | pá-tí-sèht | ປະຕິເສດ |
| region | khŏng-khèht | ຂົງເຂດ |
| registered letter | jót-măai long tha-bịan | ຈົດໝາຍລົງທະບຽນ |
| regulation | kót la-bìap | ກົດລະບຽບ |
| relationship | khwáam săm-phán | ຄວາມສຳພັນ |
| to relax | phak phawn | ພັກຜ່ອນ |
| religion | sàat-sá-náa | ສາສະນາ |

R

DICTIONARY

| | | |
|---|---|---|
| to remember | jeu | ຈື່ |
| remote | thu-la kạn-dạan | ທຸລະກັນດານ |
| rent | khaa sao | ຄ່າເຊົ່າ |
| to rent | sao | ເຊົ່າ |
| to repair | pạeng | ແປງ |
| to repeat | wâo mai | ເວົ້າໃໝ່ |
| **Please repeat that.** | ká-lu-náa wâo mai | ກະລຸນາເວົ້າໃໝ່ |
| representative | tụa tháen | ຕົວແທນ |
| republic | sǎa-tháa-la-na-lat | ສາທາລະນະລັດ |
| reservation | kạan sang-jạwng | ການສັ່ງຈອງ |
| reserve | sá-ngǔan | ສະຫງວນ |
| to reserve | sang-jạwng | ສັ່ງຈອງ |
| respect | khwáam kháo-lop | ຄວາມເຄົາລົບ |
| to respect | kháo-lop | ເຄົາລົບ |
| responsibility | khwáam hap-phít-sâwp | ຄວາມຮັບຜິດຊອບ |
| rest (relaxation) | kạan phak-phawn | ການພັກຜ່ອນ |
| to rest | phak-phawn | ພັກຜ່ອນ |
| restaurant | hâan ạa-hǎan | ຮ້ານອາຫານ |
| to return | káp | ກັບ |
| **We'll return on ...** | phûak háo ja káp ... | ພວກເຮົາຈະກັບ ... |
| return ticket | pîi pại-káp | ປີ້ໄປກັບ |
| rich | hang | ຮັ່ງ |
| right (not left) | bêuang khwǎa | ເບື້ອງຂວາ |
| on/to the right | tháang khwǎa | ທາງຂວາ |
| right (correct) | thèuk | ຖືກ |
| **I'm right.** | khàwy thèuk | ຂ້ອຍຖືກ |

| | | |
|---|---|---|
| **risk** | siang | ສ່ຽງ |
| **river** | mae nâm | ແມນ້ຳ |
| **road** | tháang | ທາງ |
| **robber** | nak-pûn | ນັກປຸ້ນ |
| **robbery** | kạan pûn | ການປຸ້ນ |
| **roof** | lăng-kháa | ຫຼັງຄາ |
| **room (general)** | hàwng | ຫ້ອງ |
| **room (hotel)** | hàwng phak | ຫ້ອງພັກ |
| **rope** | sêuak | ເຊືອກ |
| **round** | wóng món | ວົງມົນ |
| **rubbish** | khìi nyèua | ຂີ້ເຫຍື້ອ |
| **ruins** | sàak sá-lak-hak-pháng | ສາກສະລັກຮັກພັງ |
| **rule** | la-bìap | ລະບຽບ |

# S

| | | |
|---|---|---|
| **sad** | sào | ເສົ້າ |
| **safe (adj)** | pàwt-phái | ປອດໄພ |
| **safe** | tûu sep | ຕູ້ເຊັບ |
| **safely** | dûay khwáam pàwt-phái | ດ້ວຍຄວາມປອດໄພ |
| **safety** | khwáam pàwt-phái | ຄວາມປອດໄພ |
| **same** | khéu-kạn | ຄືກັນ |
| **to say** | wâo | ເວົ້າ |

| | | |
|---|---|---|
| **I said ...** | khàwy dâi wâo ... | ຂ້ອຍໄດ້ເວົ້າ ... |
| **Can you say that again?** | jâo wâo mai dâi baw | ເຈົ້າເວົ້າໃໝ່ໄດ້ບໍ່ |

| | | |
|---|---|---|
| **scenery** | thíu-that | ທິວທັດ |
| **school** | hóhng hían | ໂຮງຮຽນ |
| **secret (adj)** | lap | ລັບ |
| **secret** | khwáam lap | ຄວາມລັບ |
| **to see** | hĕn | ເຫັນ |

| | | |
|---|---|---|
| **I see. (understand)** | khàwy khào jại | ຂ້ອຍເຂົ້າໃຈ |
| **I see (it).** | khàwy hĕn | ຂ້ອຍເຫັນ |

| | | |
|---|---|---|
| selfish | hĕn kae tụa | ເຫັນແກ່ຕົວ |
| to sell | khăai | ຂາຍ |

| | | |
|---|---|---|
| Do you sell ...? | jâo khăai ... baw | ເຈົ້າຂາຍ ... ບໍ່ |

| | | |
|---|---|---|
| to send | song | ສົ່ງ |
| sentence (grammar) | pá-yòhk | ປະໂຫຍກ |
| serious | nák-nă | ໜັກໜາ |
| several | lăai | ຫຼາຍ |
| shade | hom | ຮົມ |
| share | hùn | ຫຸ້ນ |
| to share | baeng kạn | ແບ່ງກັນ |
| she | láo | ລາວ |
| shoes | kòep | ເກີບ |
| shop | hâan khâa | ຮ້ານຄ້າ |
| short (length, duration) | sàn | ສັ້ນ |
| a short time ago | waang măw măw nîi | ຫວ່າງໝໍ່ໆນີ້ |
| short (height) | tîa | ເຕັ້ຍ |
| shortage | khàat khŏen | ຂາດເຂີນ |
| to shout | hâwng | ຮ້ອງ |
| to show | sá-dạeng | ສະແດງ |

| | | |
|---|---|---|
| Show me, please. | ạo hài khàwy boeng dae | ເອົາໃຫ້ຂ້ອຍເບິ່ງແດ່ |

| | | |
|---|---|---|
| shut (adj) | pít lâew | ປິດແລ້ວ |
| to shut | pít | ປິດ |
| shy | ạai | ອາຍ |
| sick | khài | ໄຂ້ |
| sickness | lôhk | ໂລກ |
| sign | pâai | ປ້າຍ |
| signature | láai sén | ລາຍເຊັນ |
| similar | khâai khéu kạn | ຄ້າຍຄືກັນ |
| since (from that time) | tang tae | ຕັ້ງແຕ່ |

| | | |
|---|---|---|
| since (because) | neuang jàak waa | ເນື່ອງຈາກວ່າ |
| single (unmarried) | sòht | ໂສດ |
| sister | nâwng săo | ນ້ອງສາວ |
| to sit | nang | ນັ່ງ |

| | | |
|---|---|---|
| Sit down. | nang lóng | ນັ່ງລົງ |

| | | |
|---|---|---|
| situation | sá-phâap-kạan | ສະພາບການ |
| size | khá-nàat | ຂະໜາດ |
| sleep | kạan náwn | ການນອນ |
| to sleep | náwn | ນອນ |

| | | |
|---|---|---|
| I'm asleep. | khàwy kạm-láng náwn | ຂ້ອຍກຳລັງນອນ |
| He's asleep. | láo náwn lap | ລາວນອນລັບ |
| Are you asleep? | jâo náwn lap baw | ເຈົ້ານອນລັບບໍ່ |

| | | |
|---|---|---|
| sleepy | hĭu náwn | ຫິວນອນ |

| | | |
|---|---|---|
| I'm sleepy. | khàwy hĭu náwn | ຂ້ອຍຫິວນອນ |

| | | |
|---|---|---|
| slow | sâa | ຊ້າ |
| slowly | sâa | ຊ້າ |
| small | nâwy | ນ້ອຍ |
| smell | kin | ກິ່ນ |
| to smell | dọm | ດົມ |
| snow | hí-ma | ຫິມະ |
| soap | sá-bụu | ສະບູ |
| solid (adj) | nă̆a nâen; khăeng | ໜາແໜ້ນ; ແຂງ |
| some | bạang | ບາງ |
| someone | bạang khón | ບາງຄົນ |

| something | bạang yaang | ບາງຢ່າງ |
|---|---|---|
| sometimes | bạang khâng | ບາງຄັ້ງ |
| son | lûuk sáai | ລູກຊາຍ |
| song | phéhng | ເພງ |

| Sorry! | khǎw thôht | ຂໍໂທດ |
|---|---|---|

| so-so | thám-ma-dạa | ທຳມະດາ |
|---|---|---|
| soon | nái wái-wái nîi | ໃນໄວໆນີ້ |
| south | tâi | ໃຕ້ |
| souvenir | khǎwng khwǎn | ຂອງຂວັນ |
| to speak | wâo | ເວົ້າ |
| special | phi-sèht | ພິເສດ |
| spirits (alcohol) | lào | ເຫຼົ້າ |
| sport | kí-láa | ກິລາ |
| spring (season) | la-dụu bạan mai | ລະດູບານໃໝ່ |
| square | já-tú-lat | ຈະຕຸລັດ |
| stairway | khàn dại | ຂັ້ນໄດ |
| stamp | sá tạem | ສະແຕມ |
| standard (adj) | mâat-tá-thǎan | ມາດຕະຖານ |
| station (bus) | sá-thǎa-níi (lot) | ສະຖານີ (ລົດ) |
| stay | kạan phak háem | ການພັກແຮມ |

I'll stay here for (two days).
khàwy já phak yuu nîi (sǎwng mêu) ຂ້ອຍຈະພັກຢູ່ນີ້ (ສອງມື້)

| to stay | phak | ພັກ |
|---|---|---|
| to steal | lak | ລັກ |

| My money has been stolen. | ngóen khàwy thèuk lak | ເງິນຂ້ອຍຖືກລັກ |
|---|---|---|

| | | |
|---|---|---|
| **stop** | bawn jàwt | ບ່ອນຈອດ |
| **to stop** | yut | ຢຸດ |
| **storey** | sân | ຊັ້ນ |
| **ground floor** | sân lum | ຊັ້ນລຸ່ມ |
| **storm** | pháa-nyu | ພາຍຸ |
| **story** | ni-tháan | ນິທານ |
| **straight** | seu | ຊື່ |
| **straight ahead** | seu pại | ຊື່ໄປ |
| **strange** | pàek | ແປກ |
| **stranger** | khón pàek nàa | ຄົນແປກໜ້າ |
| **street** | thá-nŏn | ຖະໜົນ |
| **on strike** | pá-thûang | ປະທ້ວງ |
| **strong** | khăeng háeng | ແຂງແຮງ |
| **student** | nak-séuk-săa | ນັກສຶກສາ |
| **stupid** | ngoh | ໂງ່ |
| **suddenly** | ká-than-hăn | ກະທັນຫັນ |
| **suitcase** | ká-pao | ກະເປົາ |
| **summer** | la-dụu hâwn | ລະດູຮ້ອນ |
| **sun** | ṭaa-wén | ຕາເວັນ |
| **sure (certain)** | nae jại | ແນ່ໃຈ |

| | | |
|---|---|---|
| **Are you sure?** | jâo nae jại baw | ເຈົ້າແນ່ໃຈບໍ່ |
| **I'm sure.** | khàwy nae jại | ຂ້ອຍແນ່ໃຈ |

| | | |
|---|---|---|
| **surname** | náam sá-kụn | ນາມສະກຸນ |
| **surprise** | pá-làat jại | ປະຫລາດໃຈ |
| **sweet** | wăan | ຫວານ |
| **sweets (candy)** | khào-nŏm | ເຂົ້າໜົມ |
| **to swim** | láwy nâm | ລອຍນ້ຳ |

# T

| | | |
|---|---|---|
| **table** | tó | ໂຕະ |
| **to take** | ạo | ເອົາ |

| | | |
|---|---|---|
| **I'll take one.** | khàwy já ạo ạn neung | ຂ້ອຍຈະເອົາອັນໜຶ່ງ |
| **Can I take this?** | khàwy ạo ạn nîi dâi baw | ຂ້ອຍເອົາອັນນີ້ໄດ້ບໍ່ |

| | | |
|---|---|---|
| **to talk** | wâo | ເວົ້າ |
| **tall** | sǔung | ສູງ |
| **tasty** | sâep | ແຊບ |
| **tax** | pháa-sǐi | ພາສີ |
| **taxi** | lot thaek-síi | ລົດແທັກຊີ |
| **teacher** | náai khúu | ນາຍຄູ |
| **telephone** | thóh-la-sáp | ໂທລະສັບ |
| **to telephone** | thóh-la-sáp | ໂທລະສັບ |
| **telephone book** | pêum thóh-la-sáp | ປື້ມໂທລະສັບ |
| **temperature** | ụn-na-phúum | ອູນນະພູມ |
| **tent** | phàa tên | ຜ້າເຕັ້ນ |
| **to thank** | khǎw khàwp jại | ຂໍຂອບໃຈ |

| | | |
|---|---|---|
| **Thank you.** | khàwp jại | ຂອບໃຈ |

| | | |
|---|---|---|
| **theatre** | hóhng la-kháwn | ໂຮງລະຄອນ |
| **there** | yuu hàn | ຢູ່ຫັ້ນ |
| **they** | phûak khǎo | ພວກເຂົາ |
| **thick** | nǎa | ໜາ |
| **thief** | jọhn | ໂຈນ |
| **thin** | bạang | ບາງ |
| **to think** | khit | ຄິດ |
| **thirst** | hǐw nâm | ຫິວນ້ຳ |

| | | |
|---|---|---|
| **I'm thirsty.** | khàwy hǐw nâm | ຂ້ອຍຫິວນ້ຳ |

| | | |
|---|---|---|
| **ticket** | pîi | ປີ້ |
| **time** | wéh-láa | ເວລາ |

| | | |
|---|---|---|
| **What time is it?** | wéh-láa ják móhng | ເວລາຈັກໂມງ |
| **I don't have time.** | khàwy baw míi wéh-láa | ຂ້ອຍບໍ່ມີເວລາ |

**timetable** táa-láang wéh-láa ຕາລາງເວລາ

**tin opener** kheuang khǎi ká-pạwng ເຄື່ອງໄຂກະປອງ

**tip (gratuity)** ngóen thip ເງິນທິບ

**tired** meuay ເໝື່ອຍ

**today** mêu-nîi ມື້ນີ້

**together** phâwm kạn ພ້ອມກັນ

**toilet** hàwng nâm ຫ້ອງນ້ຳ

**toilet paper** jîa hàwng nâm ເຈ້ຍຫ້ອງນ້ຳ

**tomorrow** mêu-eun ມື້ອື່ນ

**tonight** khéun nîi ຄືນນີ້

**too (also)** dûay ດ້ວຍ

**too (as in 'too hot')** phôht ໂພດ

**tooth** khàew ແຂ້ວ

**torch (flashlight)** fái sǎai ໄຟສາຍ

**to touch** jáp ຈັບ

**to tour** thawng thiaw ທ່ອງທ່ຽວ

> **I'm touring Laos.** khàwy kạm-láng thawng thiaw yuu pá-thêht láo ຂ້ອຍກຳລັງທ່ອງທ່ຽວຢູ່ປະເທດລາວ

**tourist** nak thawng thiaw ນັກທ່ອງທ່ຽວ

**towards** thŏeng ເຖິງ

**towel** phàa set tọh ຜ້າເຊັດໂຕ

**town** méuang ເມືອງ

**track (path)** tháang ທາງ

**in transit** dọen tháang phaan ເດີນທາງຜ່ານ

**to translate** pạe ແປ

**translation** kạan pạe ການແປ

**trekking** dọen paa ເດີນປ່າ

**trip** thìaw ຖ້ຽວ

**true** thèuk tâwng ຖືກຕ້ອງ

**to trust** seua ເຊື່ອ

**to try (attempt)** pha-nyáa-nyáam ພະຍາຍາມ

**to try (taste food)** síim ຊີມ

**to try on (clothing)** láwng nung kheuang ລອງໜຸ່ງເຄື່ອງ

**TV** thóh-la-that ໂທລະທັດ

# U

| | | |
|---|---|---|
| umbrella | khán hom | ຄັນຮົ່ມ |
| uncomfortable | baw sá-dùak | ບໍ່ສະດວກ |
| under | tâi/ kâwng | ໃຕ້/ກ້ອງ |
| to understand | khào jại | ເຂົ້າໃຈ |

| | | |
|---|---|---|
| I don't understand. | khàwy baw khào jại | ຂ້ອຍບໍ່ເຂົ້າໃຈ |
| Do you understand? | jâo khào jại baw | ເຈົ້າເຂົ້າໃຈບໍ່ |

| | | |
|---|---|---|
| unemployed | wàang ngáan | ຫວ້າງງານ |
| university | ma-hăa-wi-tha-nyáa-lái | ມະຫາວິທະຍາໄລ |
| unsafe | baw pàwt-phái | ບໍ່ປອດໄພ |
| until | jọn thŏeng | ຈົນເຖິງ |
| up | khèun | ຂຶ້ນ |
| upstairs | sân thóeng | ຊັ້ນເທິງ |
| urgent | duan | ດ່ວນ |
| useful | pẹn pá-nyòht | ເປັນປະໂຫຍດ |
| useless | baw míi pá-nyòht | ບໍ່ມີປະໂຫຍດ |

# V

| | | |
|---|---|---|
| vacation (holiday) | phak tháang kạan | ພັກທາງການ |
| vaccination | sak-yáa-pâwng-kạn lôhk | ຊັກຢາປ້ອງກັນໂລກ |
| in vain | het tae baw dâi hap phŏn | ເຮັດແຕ່ບໍ່ໄດ້ຮັບຜົນ |
| valuable | míi khaa | ມີຄ່າ |
| value | láa-kháa | ລາຄາ |
| various | taang-taang | ຕ່າງໆ |
| vegetable garden | sŭan phák | ສວນຜັກ |
| vegetarian (person) | khón kịn jẹh | ຄົນກິນເຈ |
| vegetarian (adj) | jẹh | ເຈ |
| very | lăai | ຫຼາຍ |
| video | wíi-dịi-ọh | ວີດີໂອ |
| view | thíu-thát | ທິວທັດ |
| village | muu bâan | ໝູ່ບ້ານ |
| visa | wi-sáa | ວີຊາ |

| | | |
|---|---|---|
| to visit | nyîam-nyáam | ຢ້ຽມຢາມ |
| to vomit | hâak | ຮາກ |
| to vote | lêuak tâng | ເລືອກຕັ້ງ |



# W

| | | |
|---|---|---|
| to wait | láw thàa | ລໍຖ້າ |
| **Wait a moment!** | thàa béut neung | ຖ້າບຶດໜຶ່ງ |
| waiter | dék sòep | ເດັກເສີບ |
| walk | nyaang | ຍ່າງ |
| to walk | nyaang | ຍ່າງ |

**Do you want to go for a walk?**
jâo yàak pại nyaang lîin baw — ເຈົ້າຢາກໄປຍ່າງຫຼີ້ນບໍ່

| | | |
|---|---|---|
| to want | tâwng-kạan/yàak | ຕ້ອງການ/ຢາກ |
| **I want ...** | khàwy tâwng-kạan ... | ຂ້ອຍຕ້ອງການ ... |
| **We want ...** | phûak háo tâwng-kạan ... | ພວກເຮົາຕ້ອງການ... |
| **Do you want ...?** | jâo tâwng-kạan ... baw | ເຈົ້າຕ້ອງການ ... ບໍ່ |
| war | sŏng-kháam | ສົງຄາມ |
| warm | óp-un | ອົບອຸ່ນ |
| to wash (oneself) | àap-nâm | ອາບນ້ຳ |
| **I have to wash (bathe).** | khàwy tâwng àap-nâm | ຂ້ອຍຕ້ອງອາບນ້ຳ |
| to wash (clothes) | sak | ຊັກ |
| to wash (other objects) | lâang | ລ້າງ |

| | | |
|---|---|---|
| watch | kąan dųu-láe | ການດູແລ |
| to watch | boeng | ເບິ່ງ |
| **Watch out!** | la-wáng | ລະວັງ |
| water | nâm | ນ້ຳ |
| way | tháang | ທາງ |
| WC | hàwng nâm | ຫ້ອງນ້ຳ |
| we | phûak háo | ພວກເຮົາ |
| wealthy | hang míi | ຮັ່ງມີ |
| weather | ąa-kàat | ອາກາດ |
| wedding | ngáan taeng-ngáan | ງານແຕ່ງງານ |
| week | ąa-thit | ອາທິດ |
| well | nâm sàang | ນ້ຳສ້າງ |
| **Welcome!** | nyín dįi tâwn hap | ຍິນດີຕ້ອນຮັບ |
| west | thit tąa-wén tók | ທິດຕາເວັນຕົກ |
| wet | pĮak | ປຽກ |
| what | nyăng | ຫຍັງ |
| **What time is it?** | jak móhng | ຈັກໂມງ |
| **What did you say?** | jâo wâo nyăng | ເຈົ້າເວົ້າຫຍັງ |
| when | wéh-láa dąi | ເວລາໃດ |
| where | yuu săi | ຢູ່ໃສ |
| **Which way?** | tháang dąi | ທາງໃດ |
| who | phăi | ໃຜ |
| **Who do I ask?** | khàwy ja thăam phăi | ຂ້ອຍຈະຖາມໃຜ |
| wife | mía | ເມຍ |
| to win | sa-na | ຊະນະ |

W

| | | |
|---|---|---|
| window | pawng îam | ປ່ອງອ້ຽມ |
| winter | la-dụu nǎo | ລະດູໜາວ |
| wise | hûu lǎai | ຮູ້ຫຼາຍ |
| wish | kạan ạa-thí-thǎan | ການອາທິຖານ |
| to wish | ạa-thí-thǎan | ອາທິຖານ |
| with | káp | ກັບ |
| within | pháai-nái | ພາຍໃນ |
| without | pạa-sá-jàak | ປາສະຈາກ |
| woman | mae nyíng | ແມ່ຍິງ |
| wooden | het dûay mâi | ເຮັດດ້ວຍໄມ້ |
| work | wîak | ວຽກ |
| to work | het wîak | ເຮັດວຽກ |
| world | lôhk | ໂລກ |
| worse (adj) | sua kwaa | ຊົ່ວກ່ວາ |
| worse (adv) | hâai-háeng-kwaa | ຮ້າຍແຮງກ່ວາ |
| write | khǐan | ຂຽນ |

| | | |
|---|---|---|
| I'm writing ... | khàwy kạm-láng khǐan ... | ຂ້ອຍກຳລັງຂຽນ ... |
| She's writing ... | láo kạm-láng khǐan ... | ລາວກຳລັງຂຽນ ... |

| | | |
|---|---|---|
| wrong | phít phâat | ຜິດພາດ |

| | | |
|---|---|---|
| You're wrong. | jâo phít | ເຈົ້າຜິດ |

## Y

| | | |
|---|---|---|
| year | pịi | ປີ |
| two years ago | sǎwng pii kawn | ສອງປີກ່ອນ |
| yes | maen | ແມ່ນ |
| yesterday | mêu-wáan nîi | ມື້ວານນີ້ |
| you (sg) | jâo | ເຈົ້າ |
| you (pl) | phûak jâo | ພວກເຈົ້າ |
| young | num | ໜຸ່ມ |

## Z

| | | |
|---|---|---|
| zone | khèht | ເຂດ |
| zoo | sǔan sát | ສວນສັດ |
| zodiac | hǒh-láa-sàat | ໂຫລາສາດ |

DICTIONARY

# INDEX

## A



## B



## C

## H



## I



## J



## L



## M



## N



## O



## P

## R



## S



## T



## V



## W

NOTES

## SIGNS

| | |
|---|---|
| ຮ້ອນ | HOT |
| ເຢັນ | COLD |
| ທາງເຂົ້າ | ENTRANCE |
| ທາງອອກ | EXIT |
| ເປີດ | OPEN |
| ອັດ/ປິດ | CLOSED |
| ຫ້າມເຂົ້າ | NO ENTRY |
| ຫ້າມສູບຢາ | NO SMOKING |
| ຫ້າມ | PROHIBITED |
| ຫ້ອງນ້ຳ | TOILETS |